# An Egyptian Panorama

Reports from the 19th Century British Press

# An Egyptian Panorama

## Reports from the 19th Century British Press

Edited by
NICHOLAS WARNER

ZEITOUNA

Boraïe, Shaalan & Co., Publishers
13 Mariette Pasha Street, Cairo, Egypt

Original text copyright Nicholas Warner
Published 1994
Printed in Egypt
98 97 96 95 94    5 4 3 2 1

ISBN 977-5170-04-4
Dar el-Kutub № 7848/94

# Contents

*List of llustrations*                                                                viii

*Preface*                                                                            xiii

*Introduction*    MAKING THE NEWS
                  Words                                                               xv
                  Images                                                              xx

*Part One*        VIEWS OF THE PAST                                                    1
                  Tourism                                                              3
                  Exhibitions                                                         17
                  Archaeology                                                         27

*Part Two*        DAILY LIFE                                                          39
                  People                                                              41
                  Places                                                             49
                  Events                                                             55

*Part Three*      THE CRISIS IN EGYPT                                                 69
                  Royalty                                                             71
                  Suez                                                                83
                  Occupation                                                          95

*Appendix*        CHRONOLOGY                                                         115

# Illustrations

*Preface*

    Public Letter Writer  (*ILN*, September 30, 1882)          xiii

*Introduction*    MAKING THE NEWS

    The *Illustrated London News'* Steam Printing Press  (*ILN*, December 2, 1843)    xiv

    Eastern Storyteller  (*ILN*, March 18, 1854)    xv

    Mr. Albert Smith's Entertainment  (*ILN*, June 8, 1850)    xvi

    Casting the Bronze Sphinxes for Cleopatra's Needle  (*ILN*, April 16, 1881)    xvii

    The Practice of Wood Engraving  (*ILN*, July 6, 1844)    xx

    Gravers  (*ILN*, July 6, 1844)    xxi

    Lamp; Burnisher and Dauber  (*ILN*, July 6, 1844)    xxi

    Our Artist Come to Grief  (*ILN*, November 22, 1884)    xxii

    How We have To Work  (*ILN*, November 22, 1884)    xxii

    Lecture by Mr. Melton Prior  (*ILN*, March 3, 1883)    xxiii

    An "On-the-Spot" Sketch  (*ILN*, July 9, 1882)    xxiii

    Mr. Bedford, Photographist, at Philae  (*ILN*, May 16, 1862)    xxiv

*Part One*    VIEWS OF THE PAST

    Smoking Pavilion at Shepheard's Hotel  (The *Graphic*, December 11, 1880)    3

    Sketch on the Verandah at Suez    4

    Crossing the Isthmus of Suez    5

    Shepheard's Hotel    6

    Saloon of the Dahabieh or Nile Boat    7

    Dahabieh or Nile Boat    7

    Starting for the Pyramids    8

    Step Pyramid of Sakkarah, Sphinx, and Pyramids at Giza    9

    Emperor of Austria Ascending the Great Pyramid    10

Tourists Ascending the Great Pyramid 11

Bazaar at Cairo 12

Fair Iconoclasts in Egypt 13

Karnak 14

Luxor and Philae 15

Front of the Great Temple at Abu Simbel 16

Egyptian Court in Progress  (*ILN*, April 15, 1854) 17

Colossal Figures from Abu Simbel 18

Entrance to the Egyptian Court 19

Entrance to the Tomb of Beni Hassan 20

Reception of the Viceroy at the Crystal Palace 21

Collection of Egyptian Animals 22

Congress of Orientalists 23

Great Egyptian Gallery 24

Egyptian Room at the British Museum 25

Museum of Sir John Soane 26

Royal Mummies  (*ILN*, February 4, 1882) 27

Cleopatra's Needle Being Examined by Sir James Alexander 29

Cleopatra's Needle: An Illustrated History 30–31

Abandonment of Cleopatra's Needle 32

Machinery for Placing the Obelisk 33

Egyptian Sphinx 34

Discoveries at the Brick Pyramids of Dahchour 35–37

*Part Two*      DAILY LIFE

Third Class Railway Carriage  (*ILN*, March 25, 1882) 41

Musicians Performing at Coffee House 42

Courtyard of a House 43

Barber's Shop 44

People of Egypt 45

Marriage in Cairo 46

Howling Dervishes in Old Cairo 47

Ploughing in Lower Egypt    48

Entrance to the Citadel  (*ILN*, October 1, 1881)    49

Slave Market, Cairo    50

Street in Cairo    51

Rue de l'Hôtel Shepheard    52

Palace of Gezeereh    53

Interior of the Mosque of El-Azhar    54

Dromedary Race  (*ILN*, February 13, 1869)    55

Races at Cairo    56

Doseh    57

Festival of Gebr-el-Haleeg; Breaking the Canal    59

Scene at the Mohammedan Festival of the Bairam    61

Procession of the Holy Carpet    62

Dispatching the Mahmal    63

Remains of the Railway Embankment    64

Cholera in Egypt    65

Prince and Princess of Wales in Egypt    66

Turkish Sultan's Progress Through Cairo    67

*Part Three*      THE CRISIS IN EGYPT

Summer Railway Carriage for the Viceroy  (*ILN*, May 29, 1858)    71

Mohammed Ali Giving Audience    72

Reform Club Banquet for Ibrahim Pasha    73

His Highness Abbas Pasha, Viceroy of Egypt    74

Launch of Iron Steam Yacht *Faid Gihaad*    75

His Highness Said Pasha and Koenig Bey    76

Bathing Kiosk for the Viceroy of Egypt    77

Ismail Pasha and the Consuls    78

Ismail Pasha, Viceroy of Egypt    79

Reception of Tewfik at the Citadel    80

Mohammed Tewfik    81

Abbas Pasha    82

Princess Emineh Hanem                                              82

Panorama of the Harbour at Suez   (*ILN*, April 17, 1869)         83

Suez Canal Works                                                  84

Workmen Loading Dromedaries                                       85

Ismailia and the Freshwater Canal                                 86

Festival at Ismailia                                              87

Empress of the French at Ismailia                                 88

Blessing the Canal at Port Said                                   89

Procession of Ships in the Suez Canal                             90

Breakwater at Port Said                                           91

M. Ferdinand de Lesseps                                           92

Map of Suez Canal                                                 93

Cavalry Demonstration in the Arab Quarter   (*ILN*, October 14, 1882)   95

Khedive and Some Leaders of the National Party                    96

Political Crisis in Egypt                                         97

Rioters at Alexandria Wrecking a Shop                             98

Flight from Alexandria                                            99

Khedive on Board the HMS *Helicon*                                100

On the Look-out from the Pyramids                                 101

Bombardment of the Forts at Alexandria                            102

Burning of Alexandria                                             103

Guards as Equipped for Service                                    104

Arabi Pasha                                                       105

Battle of Tel el-Kebir                                            106

Entry of the Khedive                                              107

Ladies of the Harem Going to the Grand Review                     108

Arabi's Trial at Cairo                                            109

Camelry Drill                                                     110

Review of Camel Corps at Wadi Halfa                               111

New Egyptian Gendarmerie — Trying on a Fez                        112

# Preface

Of the multitude of images of Egypt that appeared in the illustrated press over the period 1842–1900, a selection has been made that will, it is trusted, not overly distort the balance of coverage of the time. The criteria for inclusion have varied from the simple requirement that the picture be sufficiently graphic, to the demands of historical sequence. The random appearance of such images over this interval of time has been, to a certain extent, corrected by grouping the pictures under broad categories.

Though it was tempting to preserve the random nature of their appearance by publishing them in a chronological order—a procedure which, if followed, would have highlighted the often extraordinary juxtapositions of imagery that occurred—it was ultimately decided to group them for ease of access. A minimum of editing has been employed on the text, but since the Victorians were never noted for their brevity, the axe has had to fall occasionally, though hopefully with discrimination. What remains should be ample for the reader to gain period flavour, however distasteful that may often be. The original spelling of words in Arabic has been preserved. The choice to consider the text and the pictures separately in the Introduction may seem arbitrary, but it was intended to establish by this dichotomy a dialogue between form and technique.

I became interested in this material while researching an altogether different subject, so it is with some embarrassment that I record my thanks to the Leverhulme Trust who supported my initial stay in Cairo. The debt of gratitude to John and Arax Warner, for collating information in London when I was abroad, and to Salima Ikram, for her valuable comments and support, can only partly be repaid by the appearance of this book.

Nicholas Warner

MONTEARD.

*The* Illustrated London News' *Steam Printing Press*

# Making the News

## *Words*

The attempt to describe Egypt has been a consistent preoccupation of those who have lived or travelled in the country since the time of Herodotus. Manetho, Diodorus Siculus and Strabo endeavoured to give a general picture of a land whose past already stretched back two and a half thousand years and whose present remained alien, enigmatic and full of latent

*The Eastern Storyteller*

knowledge. The Lady Etheria contributed her Christian understanding of Egypt, then considered part of the Holy Land. But the most exhaustive accounts are those from the Islamic period of Egypt's history. Abd al-Latif provided a visitor's view of what was, in the thirteenth century, one of

the most advanced societies in the Middle East, while the subsequent chronicles of al-Maqrizi, ibn Taghribardi, ibn Iyas and al-Jabarti provide local detail right up to the close of the eighteenth century. If the view presented in such chronicles is precise, at least as regards the Islamic past and present, the reports of Western visitors wavered between outright fancy, mere misinformation, and something that approximated to a truth that could never be wholly understood by those unfamiliar with local creeds and customs. The definitive Western appreciation of Egypt's past and present had to wait until the return to France of the survivors of Napoleon's expedition to Egypt at the beginning of the nineteenth century, and the publication of the twenty volumes that comprised the *Description de l'Egypte*.

Such was the manifold vision of Egypt, both from within and without the country, by the start of the nineteenth century. The particular view of Egypt that is presented here is not one that is found in books or chronicles. It is the view that was disseminated in the British popular press from the middle to the close of the last century. Egypt at that time was emerging into a world recently transformed by the Industrial Revolution, a revolution which Britain had initiated and continued to lead. The Industrial Revolution not only enabled the mass-production of newspapers, but also created and empowered the new middle-class that read them. Britain, more than any other European power, was able to weather this period of great upheaval and to push out the boundaries of Empire.

The physical encounter between Britain and Egypt, was complemented by a potentially more significant psychological meeting. "Oriental" Egypt had existed for centuries in the imaginative geography of Britain as a symbol of the exotic, the unknown, and therefore the dangerous. The East was a land of stories and storytellers, vividly symbolized by the tales of a *Thousand and One Nights*, while rationality and a quest for "objective truth" supposedly characterized the West. Thus, although the image of Egypt had been redrawn in the narratives of travellers and the reports of Napoleon's *savants*, it was due for a major reinvention under the new conditions imposed by the mid-nineteenth century.

One of the principal representational tools used in this reinvention was the newspaper. From their origins in sixteenth century occasional pamphlets dealing with politics, murders, and miracles, newspapers developed by the end of the eighteenth century into those that concentrated almost entirely on political journalism, and those that accommodated foreign, domestic, and commercial news. Following the triumph of encyclopaedism at the close of the century, the trend seems to have been to amalgamate these distinct strands to provide a single universal picture that was a summation of knowledge of the contemporary world order. This was paradoxical in as much as stamp taxes and paper taxes — which could be considered as taxes on knowledge itself — continued to be applied until the middle of the next century. Their removal lead to an increase in the number of papers printed, and a corresponding increase in the size of

*Mr. Albert Smith's Entertainment at Willis' Rooms*

the audience reached. The principle of encyclopaedism — to contain all knowledge in a single book — was a profound one; although the task of compiling an archaeology of the past was hard, constructing an archaeology of the present was even harder. Yet the attempt at universalism was made. "Here we make our bow, determined to keep continually before the eye of the world a living and moving panorama of all its activities and influences," wrote the editor of the *Illustrated London News* when embarking on this venture. His expressed intention is worth examination. The use of the word *panorama* in this context is instructive as it gives the key to a certain artificiality in the whole enterprise. It seems as if it is not the world and its activities that are being viewed, but a *representation* of those activities in the panorama. The contemporary invention of the panorama, diorama, or cosmorama — to name but three of these large scale mechanisms to imitate the world by technical means, including the different times of day — was wildly popular.

*Casting the Bronze Sphinxes for Cleopatra's Needle*

When accompanied by a specialist commentator such as the then renowned Albert Smith, one not only had moving pictures, but talking pictures.

And what was the audience for the universal newspaper? Nothing less than the World in the person of Mr. Everyman, a morality play figure who experienced a revival in an age much concerned with the theme of the common man. The convenience of combining pictures and commentary within newspapers proved tremendously successful. The now-portable world came to Mr. Everyman on the printed page every week, while he sat at home in the interior in which, to quote Walter Benjamin, "he assembled the distant in space and time. His drawing-room was a box in the world-theatre." His craving for spectacle was extended even to the mechanics of production, as seen in the theatrical scene of *Casting the Bronze Sphinxes for Cleopatra's Needle*.

The context in which such papers were produced was Britain at the zenith of her imperial power. Wherever traders had led to profit, armies followed to conquer, and administrators came to rule. Pax Britannica could not be lightly questioned. Within the expanse of the Empire, the specific drama with which this book deals is set in Egypt, and it unfolded in tandem with the development of the illustrated newspapers — from the arrival of the first significant numbers of Europeans in Egypt under Mohammed Ali to the Occupation and its aftermath.

In the context of universalism, Egypt could only reasonably expect to be given a small space — perhaps lodged in the dense columns of newsprint between "Science Jottings," and "Anecdotal Europe," reviews of new novels and paintings, advertisements for Dr. Scott's Electric Hairbrush and Schweitzer's Anti Dyspeptic Cocoatina, and articles on "The Excitability of Plants" or "Homicide on the Brighton Railway." But Egypt was somehow different, not to say novel: while Egypt received the normal flux of coverage dependent on wars and celebrity visits throughout the century, there was also a steady undercurrent of interest displayed in the country. This interest was partly due to the fascination of her past which was becoming increasingly accessible, and partly due to the fact that to gain access to that past a degree of exposure to the present was unavoidable. In the wider topographic and political context, she became a place of transit initially to points east, and subsequently to points south. This was to guarantee her loss of independence—not just what she was, but where she was.

Of the illustrated journals of the nineteenth century, the *Illustrated London News* was undoubtedly the most famous, as well as the oldest. Together with *Punch,* it formed the two pillars of Victorian middle-class readership. Eminently respectable, partly because in its early days it relied upon a healthy subscription from the Churchmen of England for its. survival, it always remained at arm's length from "vulgar poverty." It was established by a young printer, Herbert Ingram, who had noticed that whenever the Fleet Street papers included a picture in their issue, as they occasionally did of sensational murders and remarkable events, sales rocketed. A prospectus for the new journal he proposed to launch appeared in March 1842, containing a pledge of "Thirty Engravings Every Week of the Most Interesting

Events of the Day, in Addition to Forty-Eight Columns of News," all for the price of sixpence. The paper when it appeared two months later was initially financed by the sale of a hugely popular patent medicine called Parr's Life Pills: Victorian printers often had sidelines selling pills, as this allowed them to print the packaging and advertisements. Foremost among the *Illustrated London News*' competitors was the *Graphic,* which was founded in 1869 by William Thomas. Thomas had previously worked for the older paper, but the *Graphic* was to differ in that it pretended more towards "social realism" than its predecessor. Other British publications of the latter half of the century in a similar format were the *Illustrated Times*, the *Sphere*, the *Penny Illustrated Paper*, and the *Sketch*. Abroad there was the French *L'Illustration* and *Le Monde Illustré*, the Dutch *Hollandsche Illustratie*, the German *Illustrierte Zeitung*, and the American *Leslie's Weekly* and *Harper's Weekly*. The demand for illustrated information extended beyond general newspapers to cater for special interest groups, to include professional or semi-professional magazines, and led to a great proliferation of artistic books with wood-engraved images.

The leading article in the *Illustrated London News*' first issue started thus: "We commence our political course by a distinct aversion to the very name 'party'…" In the subsequent half-century, the newspaper retained an independence of outlook within the established limits of Victorian faith and morality. The adventure of Empire and the sense of duty of the Empire builders were a consistent theme. Yet by 1882, doubt concerning the desirability and outcome of yet another British military adventure, this time in Egypt, was expressed by the *Illustrated London News'* leader writers; a doubt shared by many other writers. The editorial of the issue of August 5th of that year ran as follows:

> The theory of the English government in their present policy in Egypt is that Arabi is a mere adventurer, and that he cares nothing for the welfare of the Egyptian people. That is possibly true; but it would be unfair to deny that, in spite of himself, he represents in a rude way a sentiment which prevails largely, not only in Egypt, but in almost all Eastern countries. Orientals are slow to form an opinion as to the tendency of passing events, but they seem at last to have awakened to the conviction that the independence of the East is being steadily threatened by the encroachments of Western races. The struggle has long been going on, sometimes when its significance has not been understood; and now the issue is apparently to be finally determined. Probably Egypt will, in a political sense, receive a larger measure of freedom than she has ever enjoyed; but it is certain that, when the present troubles have been disposed of, she will become more and more subject to European ideas and manners. The same thing may be said of other Oriental countries whose inhabitants are awaiting eagerly the approaching collision of the contending forces. That the ultimate result will be for the benefit of mankind, must, we suppose, be assumed, but it would be mere vanity to assert that the complete displacement of Eastern by Western civilization will be a process attended by no disadvantages. The social condition of Europe, and even of Great Britain, is by no means so near perfection that we can afford to look forward cheerfully to the reproduction of our modes of life among peoples who have hitherto had totally different traditions. If they, too, know what it is to struggle for existence, they have not, as a rule, the extravagant European greed for gain; they are more easily contented than we; and they possess the consolations of religions in which they have more than a nominal faith. This state of things is apparently destined to pass away; but we ought not to be surprised if the East, when its enthusiasm is kindled, fights with more than its usual ardour in support of the old order.

Though not above racist generalization, this commentary at least demonstrates that there existed some appreciation of reality among the staff writers of the paper, many of whom were distinguished authors and commentators before they embarked on journalistic careers. After the Egyptian Campaign was concluded, the paper also gave space to the rhetoric of government critics such as Randolph Churchill:

> For four years this Ministry has literally waded in blood; their hands are literally dripping and reeking with blood. From massacre to massacre they march, and their course is ineffaceably stamped upon the history of the world by an ever-flowing stream of blood. How many more of England's heroes, how many more of England's best and bravest, are to be sacrificed? This, too, is shocking and horrible — the heartless indifference and callousness of the Liberal Party to narratives of slaughter and unutterable woe...

The reader of today will find the texts that accompany the images jingoistic, patronizing, and often offensive. Occasionally they are leavened by humour, sometimes deliberate and sometimes unwitting. The Victorian reader, however, must have found the confidence expressed in the superiority of British mores and technology reassuring. Appropriately enough, it was by German bombing in the Second World War that the archives of the *Illustrated London News* were largely destroyed. Yet it took more than this to destroy the memory of that "living and moving panorama of the activities and influences of the world." The memory, as far as it concerned Egypt, is what follows in these pages.

# *Images*

Since the invention of printing, pictures have accompanied text as an invaluable aid for understanding, education, and propaganda. The particular image of Egypt in the West during the early nineteenth century was dominated by two major movements. The first was encyclopaedism, manifest most clearly in that mammoth visual compendium assembled by the *savants* and *artistes* of Napoleon: the *Description de l'Egypte*. Other works similar in scope include the endeavours of John Gardiner Wilkinson and Edward William Lane to document the *Manners and Customs of the Ancient…* and *…Modern Egyptians* respectively. These were both accompanied by a profusion of illustrations, for their authors were also gifted artists. The second movement was the romantic tradition, affected in Egypt by a strong dose of oriental fantasy. David Roberts' work embodies this approach at its picturesque best. Elements of both these influences can be seen in the illustrations that were to accompany the news reports in the illustrated press. On the one hand, there was a desire to rep-

resent accurately an often prosaic reality, but on the other, there was the urge to fulfil a preconceived fantasy of Eastern exoticism. Egypt, on the evidence of the images contained in this book, provided enough material to accommodate both intentions.

Yet in 1840, the concept of illustrations printed side by side with news reports was still just as innovative as the discovery of photography at approximately the same time. In the 1820s and 1830s a number of mass circulation—cheaply printed and crudely illustrated—journals known as the "penny dreadfuls" appeared with names like the *Portfolio*, the *Hive*, the *Penny Magazine*, and *Legends of Horror*. These were directed at the artisan and the conventionally genteel alike, and as the names suggest, were very much miscellanies. The appearance of the world's first illustrated newspaper, the *Illustrated London News*, on the 14th of May 1842, continued such a tradition while representing a revolution in the quality of the popular press. These were no scurrilous broadsheets to be thrown away; rather they were destined to be bound in large, fully-indexed Morroco leather albums and to be preserved in private libraries. Today's superfluity of colour supplements and news magazines makes it harder for us to appreciate the novelty of news that was illustrated—in this case with wood engravings. (Although the photographic negative process had already been invented, the technique of printing half-tone photographs was to take

almost another half-century to perfect, leaving no alternative to this traditional method of image production.) The
first issue of the paper was advertised by 200 men with bill-
boards, consisted of sixteen pages, contained thirty-two
engravings and sold 26,000 copies. It was produced on two
large steam-powered printing machines that worked at a
rate of "2,000 perfect impressions an hour."

The success of this great venture depended upon main-
taining topicality. A major problem from the outset was the
task of finding outstanding artists and engravers to produce
the images on time. Then, as now, news was the very
lifeblood of journalism, but the speed and accuracy required
in the transmission of such information were anathema to
most artists. Furthermore, wood engraving was a dying art
practiced by a handful of craftsmen, and it was necessary to
force this laborious and time-consuming craft to meet tight
journalistic deadlines. The engravers were dependent upon
the artists. The newspaper had its own resident artist who
would not only select which illustrations would be reproduced, but would also draw them directly onto the
woodblocks. The resident artists were a special breed,
since the process of wood engraving destroyed
their original artwork drawn upon the blocks. For
the first twenty years of publication there was no
known method of applying the picture to the wood-
block except by hand.

For the purpose of wood engraving, a hard
wood such as boxwood was used. The blocks were
prepared by cutting across rather than along the grain of the
wood, and formed sections with a standard thickness. Using

the end grain of the wood had the advantage that it was
capable of being cut cleanly in all directions under equal
pressure, and of being worked with a burin which allowed
for more delicate effects than could be achieved with a
woodcutter's knife. Because of the extremely slow rate of
growth of the box tree, branches were seldom of sufficient
diameter to produce single blocks large enough for full,
double, or half page engravings. Consequently to
make up the required
area, a dozen or
more small
blocks, each accu-
rately cut and prepared, would be bolted

*Gravers*

tightly together to provide a printing surface that was
"without line, speck, or flaw."

Such carefully prepared blocks would be sent to the resident artist. Using black and white watercolour and ink he
would draw on them with amazing detail and precision,
bearing in mind that the picture, when printed, would be in
reverse. After the drawing had been executed on the made
up block, it was returned to the engraver's studio. Here, the
disadvantage inherent in the small diameter
of the box tree was brilliantly exploited.
After a master en-graver had carved
all the lines that crossed
the joints of the
made-up block, it

*Lamp; Burnisher and Dauber*

was then disassembled and
its constituent sections were distributed for completion to
different craftsmen all trained to engrave in the same style.

During the engraving process, the block was placed on a small leather bag filled with sand, allowing it to be easily turned. Outside the hours of daylight, illumination was provided by oil lamps, and the light concentrated upon the subject by shining it through a glass globe filled with water. The engraver used a watchmaker's magnifying lens clipped to one eye, and brushed white chalk into the lines cut in the block as he went along in order to assist further his vision. Once the individual sections were complete, they were reassembled, and a first proof taken. Any corrections or retouching were carried out by the master engraver before the block was deemed ready for printing. Despite such pains, it remains a characteristic of large printed wood engravings that the joints can frequently still be seen on close scrutiny. Yet the evenness of the impression and the fine quality of the engravings produced by this method is an unparalleled testimony to the engraver's skill. Unfortunately, in the early days of the illustrated newspapers, both the names of the artists and the engraver were omitted so that it is today often difficult to identify the hands that were responsible. By the division of labour, the newspaper publisher was able to complete even the most ambitious images in a relatively short space of time. The craft was organised on a workshop principle with small groups of engravers and young apprentices. The appearance of a number of illustrated journals in

*How We Have to Work*

the latter half of the nineteenth century, coupled with an increased demand for illustrated books and magazines led to the employment of large numbers of engravers and to the growth of independent studios under well known masters such as Dalziel, Whymper, and Linton.

The image itself was arrived at by a process of collage: the piecing together snippets of information—"the latest intelligence," and "on-the spot-sketches" provided by special correspondents or travelling artists—with existing pictorial reference material. Chance witnesses of important events would often send in their sketches out of a sense of public-spiritedness. As so many people were adept at drawing in the last century, the results from this seemingly unreliable method of information-col-

*Our Artist Come to Grief at the Second Cataract*

*Lecture on the Egyptian War by Mr. Melton Prior, before the Prince of Wales at the Savage Club*

send back copy of their own with the sketches. The travelling artist was expected to be in the front-line, and to tolerate a certain amount of hardship in pursuit of his subject, whether being wrecked at the Cataracts or attacked by mosquitoes. In the case of veterans—such as William Simpson and Melton Prior who both worked in Egypt for the *Illustrated London News*—they were celebrated in their own right on their return home, just as contemporary war correspondents are today. Prior even gave illustrated lectures about his experiences in Egypt covering "The Crisis of 1882." Their work was also published separately in book form with accompanying tales of the trials and tribulations they had endured in pursuit of their subjects.

Without telephone or telegraph, the artist would need to calculate when to send his drawings and watercolours so that they would arrive in London with the minimum time loss before publication. Egypt was an important staging post in the lines of communication that extended from London to the Far East. Material would pass through Suez to Cairo (before the construction of the canal), and then on to Alexandria where the connection would be made with the homeward mail to London. Here, the drawings—often covered with explanatory notes—would

lection were surprisingly successful. It was common to swap pictures with similar publications within Europe, and if the stories for which the blocks were made were not run at the time, the blocks could be stored for years until another suitable opportunity to use them arose. The best results however were achieved if the paper could despatch its own travelling artist to cover particular events abroad, normally wars. From the theatre of war, these artists would also simultaneously be able to provide local ethnographic and topographic details, and were sometimes expected to

*An "On-the-Spot" Sketch*

be delivered into the hands of the resident artist who would begin transferring them to the woodblocks, adding details when they were needed, but trying to keep to the original as much as possible. Then the blocks were sent on to the engravers before being published within a week of the arrival of the sketches in London.

*The Prince of Wales examining the negatives taken by Mr. Bedford, photographist, at Philae*

Images produced in this manner, though they may today be criticized as being stereotypical or imperialistic, remain a significant archive for the historian, and a remarkable testimony to the technological ingenuity of the age.

During the 1860s photographic prints were becoming increasingly available and initially provided the artists of the illustrated newspapers with a new source of visual reference material. This even extended to a commentary on the act of picture-taking itself, as when the artist recorded Francis Bedford taking a photograph on the occasion of the visit of the Prince of Wales to Egypt in 1862. It was, however, the photograph that was ultimately to put an end to the whole elaborate enterprise of providing wood-cut images for reproduction in the popular press. By the end of the century, half-tone reproduction was commonplace and engravings had been relegated to the advertisements of accoutrements that travellers visiting Egypt might need. The golden era of the illustrated newspapers from the point of view of hand-cut engravings thus lasted from 1840 to 1890, and looking back on this half-century the editor of the *Illustrated London News* had this to say by way of an epitaph:

Many readers of this journal can summon before their mind's eye a whole gallery of engravings which illustrate the past for him more vividly than the pen of the most graphic historian. The speeches of statesmen are forgotten, the thunder of leading articles has died away, the roll of the illustrious dead has faded from the memory, but in an instant, remembrance of a picture brings back life to buried associations.

# Part One

# Views of the Past
*Tourism, Exhibitions, Archaeology*

At the beginning of the last century, British visitors to Egypt had been, in the main, either members of the army, rich young men on an extended "grand tour," or highly motivated individuals in search of intellectual or commercial gain. The development of the Overland Route to India in the early 1840s, encouraged a much larger influx of visitors. Coincidentally, this was an event exactly contemporary with the advent of the illustrated newspapers. Though most of this journey was in fact by sea, there was an overland stage through Egypt from Alexandria to Suez via Cairo that dramatically reduced the length of the trip from Britain to India and points further East. India was, at the time, the single most prized imperial possession, while Egypt was merely a convenient staging post. The route itself was developed by a private individual, Thomas Waghorn, rather than on any government initiative, and its effect was to make Egypt increasingly available to ordinary travellers. Even those on official business were reluctant to forego a transit stop at the newly opened Shepheard's Hotel in Cairo, and a ride to see the pyramids. The more wealthy visitors might prolong their encounter by hiring a boat to take them down the Nile in relative comfort, stopping off at all the sights on the way. As one guide book of 1864 put it, "Life on a Nile barque has a charm which seldom fails to operate even on the most inert mind. The traveller is perfect king on his own boat." Soon, all necessary arrangements could be made through organised travel companies. Of most interest to tourists were the many remnants of the Pharaonic civilization, whose monuments seemed to exert a poignant attraction for those who considered themselves members of the "most energetic race on earth" as a reminder that even the greatest of empires, in time, must fall. For those in search of the curious, the exotic, and the romantic, Egypt's ruins were unparalleled.

If these tourists so desired, they could purchase some relic of that ancient past in the bazaar in Cairo before their return voyage. If not there were plenty of mementos of "King Pharaoh" at home since they lived in the Age of the World Exposition. The reconstructed Crystal Palace at Sydenham contained a number of full-scale representations of various fragments of Egyptian architecture; and who was to say the reality of the original was in any way preferable to the sight of these artifices? The display even went so far as to include the occasional live attraction. The Viceroy of Egypt, Ismail, was temporarily made a focus of popular attention on his visit to Britain in 1869, and a collection of Egyptian animals was sent to the zoological gardens in Regent's Park for public view in 1849.

The physical appropriation of Egypt's past went even further than engraving Queen Victoria's cartouche in hieroglyphs on a replica temple in the Crystal Palace. The Rosetta Stone, which made this act possible, was one of the objects brought back from Egypt and given a place of honour in the British Museum. It was here that the century's mania for codification, classification and collection reached its apotheosis in this great storehouse where objects great and small from all over the world were displayed in ranks of showcases forming a panorama of comparative cultures. And for those objects that the museum rejected, there were private buyers with personal fantasies that only the commodity fetish could fulfill.

Individual enterprise was responsible for bringing "home" even the largest pieces of Egypt's past, bequeathed to Britain by Mohammed Ali himself. The transport, (or should one say the arrangement made for its "British naturalisation,") of the obelisk dubbed "Cleopatra's Needle," was promoted and followed by the press all the way from the beach of Alexandria to the embankment of the Thames. The lure of hidden treasure provided a spur to robbers and archaeologists alike. While robbery had been commonplace for centuries, the desire to excavate for the sake of knowledge and to protect Egypt's heritage was new. The foundation of the Egyptian Museum in Boulak and the Department of Antiquities were rare positive moments in what was otherwise a century of plunder.

# Tourism

### Sketch on the Verandah at Suez
*Illustrated London News*, April 25, 1857

We arrived at Suez at a splendid hotel, with real Egyptian rooms, capital ventilation, a delicious balcony overlooking the Red Sea, of which I send you a sketch, showing the English head-dresses. Everybody has a turban around his wide-awake and a veil over that; it is the most becoming head-dress. Last night we went to a native coffee shop, with our Turkish lanterns; seated ourselves on the stone divans; ordered narghiles, and pulled away like real Turks. We all had fezzes; and, through the medium of the guide, conversed with the soldier who had come with our caravan. I never saw anything so picturesque in all my life. The whole of yesterday was spent pelting the natives from our balcony with oranges. The balcony was just above the Red Sea, which was full of boats. All day long we heard, "A boat, Sir? Want a boat, Sir? A good boat!" "Like a swim, Sir?" by semi-clothed natives. "Here, gentlemen—I say, master, take a boat?" "Here, here, want change for a sovereign?" Such were the cries I heard all day from Achmet, from Selim, from Abdallah, from Ali, *e tutti quanti.* The dinners were awfully noisy—nearly 300 people at dinner and no bells. When you want the man you clap your hands; Englishmen out of England being the merriest dogs in existence—with as many as 300 people clapping their hands at once! The poor darkies did not know where to run.

## Crossing the Isthmus of Suez

*Illustrated London News*
June 5, 1858

The gentleman to whom we are indebted for the accompanying engravings writes as follows: "When I was homeward bound—less than two years ago—the whole distance from Suez to Cairo and *vice versa* was performed in vans. Then five vans, each containing six "insides," started in a set—changed cattle at posthouses, at stages of six or seven miles, through the desert, and accomplished the journey in some seventeen or eighteen hours. Four hours after the departure of one set, another set started, and so on until the number of passengers was exhausted. Now a railway crosses the desert from Cairo to about twenty-three miles from Suez. All the cattle are collected on this space, and almost any number of vans start at once: a rare sight it is—my sketch gives a very feeble idea of the wild excitement prevailing. I would not have missed the little bit of "vanning" for a great deal; but it won't be had much longer. Soon the rail will be opened all the way to Suez; and the enterprising traveller will be able to sleep as soundly across the desert as he would from London to Brighton."

The following extract from the letter of a private soldier gives a lively picture of a portion of the Overland Route: "After partaking of an excellent breakfast, served in a canvas tent, we were provided with donkeys to cross the desert to Suez, a distance of 25 miles. Fancy about 200 Europeans in white clothing, on donkeys, followed by Arabs on foot in their many-coloured and motley garments, surrounded by vast plains and hills of nothing but sand, and you have a scene which must be witnessed to be fully appreciated. The animals jogged along between a walk, a run, and a trot, without great labour, till we had proceeded about fourteen miles, when we halted about an hour for refreshment. The weather was agreeably warm, and there was little or no wind, and no annoyance was experienced from sand. We reached Suez early in the afternoon, where we dismounted from our chargers; and, although these patient little animals had carried a load of thirteen or fourteen stone a distance of twenty-five miles, when within half a mile of their destination, most of them broke into a gallop of their own accord, and arrived with flying colours at the gates of Suez with no appearance of fatigue. The Arabs, also, who had followed barefoot at the tails of their respective animals, showed no sign of being tired. It was laughable to see some of the animals occasionally slip on their knees and pitch their riders in the sand, and but few escaped a fall or two; but no one was hurt. There were also several caravans similar to English bathing-machines, and drawn by horses and mules, but very few chose this method of crossing the desert. On reaching Suez, we were beset by the donkey drivers for *bakshish*. The Arabs and donkeys were not allowed within the gates of Suez, and would return next morning to go through the same fatigue on the following day."

## Shepheard's Hotel, Cairo
*Illustrated London News*, February 9, 1884

All English visitors to Egypt are acquainted with this establishment in the city of Cairo. It is situated in the Esbekieh quarter, which is quite modern and second-rate Parisian in style, or perhaps third-rate, having a Frenchified provincial aspect, with its square of garden and shrubbery, not much fresh verdure, its foreign hotels, restaurants, cafés, kiosks, theatre and opera house, concert-rooms, billiard-rooms, and cigar-shops. This famous hotel, to quote Mr. Broadley's description, "consists of a rambling and somewhat ruinous two-storied mansion, on the left-hand side of the street leading from the railway station to the centre of the city. Its spacious rooms surround a quadrangle, and the garden in which it stands is shaded by luxuriant palm-trees and refreshing green creepers. A short flight of steps leads you from the street into a broad and cool roofed verandah, paved with marble, into which opens the principal entrance, leading to the refreshment-bar and dining-rooms. Its steps are a limit which the clamorous donkey-boys and pedlars in the street below hardly dare to pass. The verandah of Shepheard's Hotel is something more than an ordinary lounge or pleasant site of Oriental *dolce far niente*: it is an Egyptian institution. When we hear in London that 'European opinion in Cairo is deeply moved,' that 'European opinion approves,' or that 'Anglo-Egyptian sensitiveness is outraged,' we should know that the inmates of the balcony at Shepheard's Hotel have spoken. The varied forms of easy-chair which fill that coolest of cool verandas are intimately connected with the past, present, and future of Egypt."

## Saloon of the Dahabieh or Nile Boat
*Illustrated London News*, February 27, 1869

The river barge or dahabieh, fitted up for the Prince and Princess of Wales' Nile voyage, is named the *Skandria*, or Alexandria, in compliment to her Royal Highness. Its interior forms a suite of rooms fitted up as the private apartments of the Prince and Princess during the trip up the Nile. There is no engine on board to propel this barge, nor any cooking apparatus, so that the vessel is free from many of the discomforts of steam-boat travelling. The steamer which takes the dahabieh in tow contains the accommodation for the staff; and a third steamer carries the cuisine. The interior of the dahabieh is very elegantly furnished. The divans are covered with blue silk, and a piano gives quite a drawing-room look to the saloon.

## Starting for the Pyramids
*Illustrated London News,* October 3, 1874

An Oriental tour by way of Cairo includes a picnic party to the Pyramids. Forty centuries, as Napoleon said, look down upon Smith, Brown, Jones, and Robinson, drinking their bottle of Bass in the desert, and eating "the sand which is there." These honest Britons are likely to be condemned as vulgar snobs for their lack of enthusiastic emotion in the presence of those enormous antiquities. But we do not really see the claim to extraordinary veneration here, any more than in the big amphitheatre at Rome, where sights of brutal butchery entertained the corrupt society of the Imperial metropolis. Those cruel old Pharaohs, with their

insensate pride, thinking to immortalise themselves by a foolish waste of brick and stone and human slave-labour, are not the more worthy of our respect for having lived a very long time ago. The mighty piles of exquisite masonry are indeed deserving of that kind of admiration we should give to any other great works of mechanical skill, combined with the expenditure of great public or private wealth. They prove that some portions of mankind in former ages, like some of our contemporaries, had more money than discretion to make a good use of it, and commanded the services of others who had as much cleverness, in their way, as our modern engineers and contractors. Is there any reason for our worshipping the useless bulk of such monumental buildings, in which the true charm of art—its message through the senses to the soul from the region of ideal harmonies—is totally deficient? We know not; but it is right that one should go and see the Pyramids while sojourning at Cairo. The nearest are within sight of the city, looking southwest from the ramparts of the citadel. You may ride upon donkeys, which is amusing to English ladies and gentlemen, and makes them fancy themselves quite in the East, in spite of the European luxuries of Shepheard's Hotel and the railway omnibus that conveyed them from the station yesterday. The scene represented in our large Engraving, has all the characteristics of unromantic truth. There may be good fun in this day's excursion, but not in the spirit of a pilgrimage. If you don't care to ride a donkey, as you would scorn to mount the humble beast on Hampstead Heath or at Margate, there is a carriage-and-pair at your service, for about sixteen shillings, along the good macadamised road from Boulak, on the opposite bank of the Nile, to the Great Pyramid of Giza. Hampers are to be packed as for Epsom Downs on the Derby Day. It never rains in Egypt, and who cares for King Pharaoh?

**The Great Step Pyramid of Sakkarah, the Great Sphinx, the Three Pyramids at Giza**
The *Graphic*, December 11, 1880

**The Emperor of Austria Ascending the Great Pyramid**
*Illustrated London News*, December 25, 1869

There are some places and conditions in life which seem to bring all men to the same level. We are often brought to a situation where each visible distinction or rank is lost, where we find that individual men are very much alike, and that all are really equal. The Great Pyramid is one of those places. If you wish to ascend it you are handed over to two sturdy Arabs, who seize upon you, and, for the time, you are at their mercy, your liberty of action is gone. They hold on to you and lug you up each step; they dictate to you the path and the particular stone you are to put your foot on; they push and shove you as if you were a bale of cotton. Their conversation is the latest slang of London or Paris; at least I know their English vocabulary is exclusively slang, which culminates at the top of the Pyramid when you arrive with a loud "Hip, hip, hurra!" and the most unreasonable demand for *baksheesh*. Whether they treated the Emperor of Austria to slang or not, I could not say, nor can I tell if they speak German as they do French and English; but I can truly say that the Emperor was no more of a great personage at the Pyramid than any of the crowd who now so often visit that wonderful structure. As he was pushed and pulled up over its huge stones he looked like a captive in the hands of his enemies; and he seemed for the moment to be very ill-used. Anyone would have taken him for the usual overland passenger who does the Pyramid in passing through Egypt. The visit of the Emperor took place on the 26th, and the Khedive came out at the same time. An Arab race was arranged to the top of the Pyramid and down again; and after dark the Pyramid was illuminated with fireworks.

## Tourists Ascending the Great Pyramid
*Illustrated London News,* May 7, 1887

King Khufu, or *Cheops* of the Memphite Dynasty, who built the biggest of the Pyramids at Giza above five thousand years ago, never dreamt that these English young ladies and gentlemen would clamber up its sides after breakfasting at Shepheard's Hotel in Cairo, to overlook the vast plain, the site of his royal metropolitan city. It was an impossible feat when the whole pyramid, as originally constructed, had a smooth surface of polished limestone slabs, which were long since removed, leaving the rough granite blocks, 3 or 4 feet high, now available for labori-ous climbing. Tourists who feel strong enough, with the help of Arab guides, to perform this fatiguing ascent, may enjoy the harm-less pride of having "done" it, and consider themselves in a superi-or position to that of Napoleon, as he told the French army, gather-ing below for battle with the Mamelukes that "forty centuries are looking down upon you!"

**The Bazaar at Cairo**
The *Graphic*, December 18, 1869

Egypt is a new revelation to a man who has never felt the slow pulse of Oriental life, however far and wide in Europe generally, or across the Atlantic in the Western world, his wanderings may have extended. The cloudless sky, for ever wide awake; the bright colours of costumes on every side; the grave, dark faces crowned with many folded turbans; and the figures in flowing costumes that move about; the "palms in clusters" all over the flat expanse; the slow-moving train of camels; and the villages of slate-coloured mud you come upon from time to time, all looking as if they had been brought out of the British Museum bodily—these are only a very few of the characteristics of Egypt which give a new thrill to the visitor who sees them for the first time.

Goodness knows, Cairo is not beautiful in the ordinary sense of the word. As soon as you leave the open square in the centre of the city—a dreary expanse, at one side of which, with floods of donkey-boys surging around the stone terrace in front, stands the far-famed Shepheard's Hotel—you plunge into the labyrinth of bazaars and narrow lanes of which the place consists. They are not clean, they are not handsome in their architecture, they are not convenient for foot passengers. Donkeys, and now and the men of supreme dignity on horseback are jammed together in a confusion which none but Egyptians could endure with patience for a week; but there they are, unchanged since the days—if we may use that paradoxical expression—of the Arabian Nights, and there the solemn, turbanned Oriental merchants—it would be an outrage to think of them as shopkeepers—sit cross-legged, and smoke, and show as much interest in the transaction of business as if they were carved in stone, or as if they had been preserved for our use like mummies.

The goods, as our readers may see from the sketch of a Cairo Bazaar which has been sent by our artist in Egypt, are exposed to the weather without fear, for though it is not true to say that it never rains in Cairo, it only "comes out wet" once in a hundred years or so, and the risk of a shower is not excessive. The wandering P & O passengers in search of curiosities, however, will not pick up any treasures unless they go into some little den, and bargain for an hour or so with the stolid proprietor. If they haggle long enough, and act their part properly, exhibiting indignation and disgust at the atrocious character of the articles presented for their inspection, it is possible that finally he may produce, from hidden receptacles in the rear, any really good and valuable stores he may possess; but no oriental dealer will let you see the best things first. He has any quantity of time at your service, but he has no more respect for yours than for his own.

## Fair Iconoclasts in Egypt
The *Graphic,* July 26, 1890

The increased facilities of travel on the Nile, and the fact that Egypt has become a fashionable winter resort, are factors which yearly attract an increasing number of tourists of all classes and nationalities to the shores of the historical river. For some reasons this is to be regretted. The monuments and the temples are rapidly being mutilated by relic hunters, and by Arabs encouraged by the market in this sort of commodity which the travellers foster. Unless, therefore, vigorous steps are taken without further delay, either by the Society for the Preservation of the Monuments of Ancient Egypt or by the Egyptian Government, those portions of the bas reliefs and carvings which have hitherto escaped all the vicissitudes to which they have been subjected during the various epochs of Egyptian history are destined shortly completely to disappear.

Our illustration portrays some of our fair American cousins chipping away portions of the carving on the magnificent columns of the Ptolemaic Temple of Hathor or Venus at Denderah. This temple is one of the best preserved and grandest monuments of Egypt, notwithstanding the fact that the art is in some respects inferior to that to be seen in some of the older temples. This imposing edifice is noted for having on its outer walls the supposed portrait-representations of Cleopatra and her son by Julius Caesar. This fact apparently inspires those tourists suffering from the mania for collecting mementos of their peregrinations to possess themselves of pieces of the stonework, hence, month by month, during each season the mutilations exhibit increasing depth and breadth. The fair visitors to this historical temple whom our artist caught in the act of vandalism depicted, while keeping a good lookout for the inefficient Egyptian custodian, little thought that the artist busily engaged in their vicinity was making notes for future use wherein their wanton pastime should be given publicity. We regret that truth to circumstances compels us to give the fair sex a prominence in this army of destroyers, for, as a matter of fact, it is very rarely on a sojourn on the Nile that a man is discovered engaged in this occupation, whereas certain types of ladies, who by dress and behaviour are generally found to be prominent members of the American personally-conducted parties, can constantly be seen engaged in similar work to that at which the three girls in our illustration were caught. It is to be hoped that effectual measures will soon be adopted for the protection of these relics of a bygone civilization, whose existence is not of national, but of world-wide importance. Any tourist—irrespective of sex—caught mutilating any of these wonderful monuments should meet with summary punishment. Appeals to the good taste of the travelling community are of no avail; such destruction should be considered a crime of a specially heinous nature, and be treated accordingly.

## Karnak
*Illustrated London News,* April 5, 1862

The visit of the heir apparent of the British throne, the representative of one of the most energetic races of the living present, to a land abounding with mighty memorials of the long-buried past is so full of interest, and so strangely, even sadly, suggestive, as the mind perforce glances to the future, that no apology is needed for a recurrence to the theme. Or if some excuse be thought necessary, it will be found in the Illustrations which we are enabled to give of some incidents connected with the visit of his Royal Highness to Egypt…

On the morning of Sunday the 15th, horses having been provided, the Royal party, attended by a numerous guard, visited Karnak, remaining there a whole day. After strolling about the ruins, the Prince gave directions for Divine Service to be held at eleven a.m. in the Hall of Columns. The Rev. Canon Stanley officiated, and, after prayers, delivered a most appropriate and highly interesting sermon, which would have been impressive under any circumstances, but was particularly so from the many associations it called up by the singularity of our position. At two p.m. a sumptuous lunch was in readiness, having been prepared on board the steamer and brought up to the temple in charge of M. le Chef de Cuisine and his satellites. The remainder of the day was occupied in explaining these splendid monuments of a past and almost unknown age. The sun was setting and tinging with its roseate hues every object as the Royal cavalcade emerged from amongst those immense piles of ruined palaces and temples even now the wonder and admiration of the world, and the whole scene was picturesque in the extreme.

## Luxor and Philae
*Illustrated London News,* April 12, 1862

Next in importance to the ruins of Karnak are those of the Palace of Luxor [sic], rather more than one mile above the temple, but connected with it by a *dromos* or street, commencing at an obelisk of red granite, covered with a profusion of hieroglyphics, admirably executed. The fellow obelisk to this now forms the principal ornament of the Place de la Concorde at Paris. The dimensions of the palace are less than those of the temple, but the style of architecture is considered superior, and the state of preservation is more complete. Consisting generally of the same succession of courts and gigantic columns as already described at Karnak, it is unnecessary to enter into further detail.

The island of Philae, lies in the middle of the Nile, a short way above the First Cataract. This beautiful and sacred island, with its temples and magnificent groves of palm trees, is considered as the prettiest spot in all Egypt. It is celebrated as being the burial place of Osiris, whose sepulchre is revered by the Egyptian priests. The pleasure derived from the beauty of the island is, however, considerably diminished by the filth abounding in the town, which is built of mud buildings. Ranging along one side of the island is the Temple of Isis. This temple resembles in its courts and propylae the other Egyptian fanes, but the form is extremely irregular. It is not so colossal as the edifices of Thebes. The architecture is elegant and chaste, the capitals being composed of the leaves of various plants, especially of those of the lotus, the colouring of which is beautifully fresh. The views from this island are surpassingly picturesque.

**Front of the Great Temple at Abu Simbel**
The *Graphic*, December 25, 1880

The Great Temple of Abu Simbel forms the leading attraction to the Upper Nile. The interior vast hall, carved out in the living rock, is wonderful enough. Its proportions are gigantic, and it is supported by eight Osiride columns, i.e., columns with the head and figure of Osiris, as at the Rameseum. The great marvel of all, however, is the outside; where, cut out from the face of the rock, four gigantic figures of our great Ramesses II are sitting, side by side, in a sublime repose, upon their thrones. Their total height is given at sixty-six feet. A great part of one of them, however (as the engraving shows), has been shamefully wedged out and thrown down. Everybody has remarked upon the excessive sweetness of the expression of these faces, which, taking into consideration their enormous size — the ear measuring 3 feet 5 inches — is miraculous: and to this I must add, according to my own observation, that the flat open hands, laid out upon the knees, impart a very magic of placidity. They look calmly out over a very broad part of the river. We fortunately moored there for the night, when the scene far surpassed that by day. It happened to be full moon, shining full upon them; and clambering up the enormous masses of golden sand which are banked in front of the temple, we lay there and enjoyed the magical effect which it may be imagined so fine a moonlight would cast upon those countenances.

# Exhibitions

## The Crystal Palace at Sydenham—Colossal Figures from Abu Simbel
*Illustrated London News,* July 22, 1854

When Napoleon disdainfully said, in answer to a diplomatic intimation from this country, that those who ignored the Consular Republic must be persons who would also ignore the existence of the sun in his noonday blaze, he spoke of what was certainly a very conspicuous object in the new economy of European nations. In a smaller manner, these smaller figures are conspicuous amidst the treasures of that marvellous structure which crowns the breezy heights of Sydenham.

They are reproduced from the temple of Ramesses the Great, at Abu Simbel, in Nubia, and are specimens of the sort of work on which the Egyptians were engaged by the mere potent of their kings some sixteen hundred years before the coming of the Redeemer. With the exception of "the grim and hushed repose" of Egyptian sculpture, we see in it nothing that is really noble, unless mere size is to count for such. But this is merely an abstract point; a question of taste, which of course, has nothing to do with the interest belonging to these immense figures or with the merit of those men of science and genius who have with so much labour and with such splendid success, reproduced in modern England, on the scale of the actual and true dimensions of the old Egyptian school and of all the others (extant or extinct) of human art. The heads of the figures were modeled by Mr. Joseph Bonomi, from a cast made by him during his ten years' investigatory residence in Egypt. The cast itself he has given to the British Museum.

As to the interests of the building—if the eagerness already shown by the public to visit it—be not freakish and ephemeral, but, as we believe, profound and likely to endure—there can be very little doubt of the complete ultimate success of the immense venture.

## The Crystal Palace — Entrance to the Egyptian Court
*Illustrated London News*, August 5, 1854

We approach the Egyptian Court from the Nave by an avenue of lions, cast from a pair brought back from Egypt by Lord Prudhoe, and we have before us the outer walls and columns of a temple, not taken from any one particular structure, but composed from various sources, to illustrate Egyptian columns and capitals during the Ptolemaic period, somewhere about 300 B.C. On the walls are coloured sunk-reliefs showing a king making offerings or receiving gifts from the gods. The capitals or heads of the columns are palm and lotus leaved; some showing the papyrus in its various stages of development, from the simple bud to the full-blown flower. On the frieze above the columns is a hieroglyphic inscription, stating that "in the seventeenth year of the reign of Victoria, the ruler of the waves, this Palace was erected and furnished with a thousand statues, a thousand plants, etc, like as a book for the use of men of all countries." This inscription is repeated, with some slight additions, on the frieze of the interior of the Court. On the cornice of both the inside and outside of the Court, are the names of Her Majesty and Prince Albert, engraved in hieroglyphic characters, and also winged globes, the symbolic protecting deity of doorways.

## Entrance to the Tomb of Beni Hassan
*Illustrated London News,* August 5, 1854

Passing on, we find ourselves in a dark tomb copied from one at Beni Hassan. It is the earliest piece of architecture in the Crystal Palace, its date being about 1660 B.C. The original tomb is cut into a solid chain of rocks that forms the boundary on the east side of the Nile, separating the sandy desert from the fertile valley of the river. Although architectural remains exist in Egypt of a much earlier date than this tomb, it still possesses great value to us, for it may be considered as exhibiting the first order of Egyptian columns, which was employed in constructing buildings at as remote a period as two thousand years before Christ; this fluted column in another respect claims our attention, for there can be but little doubt that it supplied the Greeks with the model of their early Doric.

## Reception of the Viceroy at the Crystal Palace
*Illustrated London News*, July 10, 1869

The grand public festival in honour of the Viceroy of Egypt at the Crystal Palace, which took place on Tuesday week, was likewise attended by the Prince and Princess of Wales, as recorded in out last. The whole vast assembly, which thronged the floor and galleries, was reckoned at 30,000 persons. There were three Royal boxes; the centre one for the Viceroy of Egypt and the Prince and Princess of Wales, sitting together, with the Duke and Duchess of Sutherland, and several of their party; the other two for different members of their suite. These boxes were splendidly fur-nished and sumptuously decorated; and so were the ante-rooms, the private corridors, and a banquet room overlooking the gardens and fountains, where the Duke of Sutherland had caused a choice repast to be prepared for the Royal party. There was a concert, which comprised some of the finest sacred music of Handel, Mendelssohn, Mozart, Rossini, and Costa, performed by an orchestra and chorus of 3,000, under the direction of Sir Michael Costa; the arrangements having been made by the Sacred Harmonic Society. At ten o'clock there was a splendid display of fireworks in the gardens, with several novel and beautiful pyrotechnic effects. This concluded the public festivities in honour of the Viceroy of Egypt.

## Collection of Egyptian Animals
*Illustrated London News*, August 4, 1849

The late Viceroy of Egypt, some months before his death, placed at the disposal of the Hon. Charles Murray, Her Majesty's Consul-General, a collection of living animals which had been obtained by His Highness' command in Nubia, and which he destined as a mark of his favour towards the Zoological Society. His Highness during his visit to this country had frequent opportunities of observing the useful influence exercised by this institution, and readily lent his aid towards increasing its means of instruction. The Council availed themselves of His Highness' liberal offer to maintain this collection in Cairo until the period had arrived which might appear most favourable for its transport to England; and they accordingly despatched in the spring of the present year a trustworthy agent to receive and attend to the animals from the time of their delivery at Alexandria, whither they were conveyed at the cost by the direction of His Highness' representatives.

In addition to this magnificent gift, the Hon. C.A. Murray succeeded in obtaining three Lions, a Cheetah, an enormous Baboon, Ostriches, Gazelles, Sultana Fowls, Pelicans, and a Flamingo; besides a collection of living Reptiles which amounted to about 70 head, and included examples of 13 species of great interest and novelty.

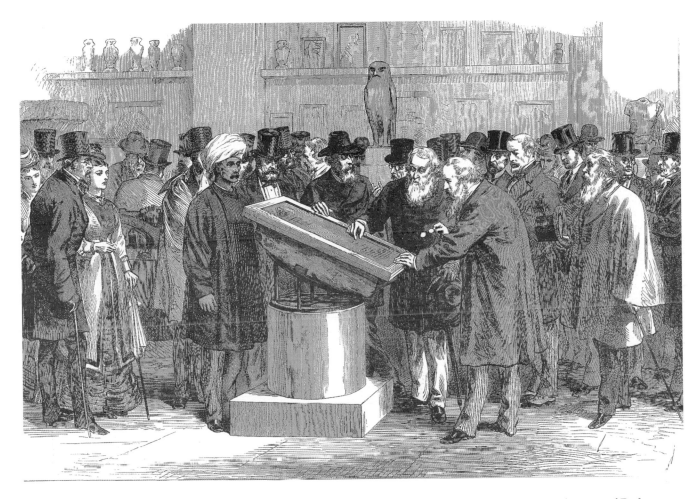

## The Congress of Orientalists
*Illustrated London News,* September 26, 1874

The second year's national Congress of Oriental scholars was held last week in London. Above one hundred learned men of acknowledged reputation, from different countries of Europe, with some deputed by the governments of Egypt and of India, attended the Congress. It was on Tuesday that Dr. Birch welcomed the Oriental scholars at the British Museum. We present a sketch of the scene witnessed upon this occasion in the Egyptian Saloon. Dr. Birch there showed his visitors the famous Rosetta stone, which was found at Rosetta, near the Western mouth of the Nile. It is inscribed with a decree in honour of Ptolemy V, one of the Greek or Macedonian kings of Egypt, about 200 years before the Christian era. The sentences are written in three different alphabets, the hieroglyphic, or sacred symbolic characters; the enchoral or demotic, which was the common popular style in Egypt; and the Greek. By this means it was that Dr. Young, M. Champollion, and other scholars of the last generation, obtained a key to the meaning of the hieroglyphics of Egypt, and the whole structure of our knowledge of the ancient history of that country has been raised on this fragment of stone.

**The Great Egyptian Gallery, the British Museum**
*Illustrated London News*, April 15, 1854

The Easter visitors to the British Museum will be gratified to find that since the last holiday gathering, the Great Egyptian Gallery has been newly arranged, as represented in the accompanying illustration. The entire length of this noble apartment is 375 feet from end to end, and is devoted to Egyptian antiquities, with the exception of one saloon, which is set apart for some of the large objects from Nineveh, and forms a striking feature in the Gallery. The alterations which have taken place in this wing of the Museum render it truly interesting. The various objects which some time since were crowded within the limits of which the large lions presented by Lord Prudhoe were the boundary, are now pleasingly displayed, ample space being allowed for the visitor to walk around them. Two rows of shelves have also been added to the walls, below the windows, to sustain the specimens of pottery and the smaller slabs with inscriptions: some of them have been put into oaken frames, and glass inserted so as to prevent further decay. Below are ranged the larger slabs and, fragments of fresco paintings: some are from tombs at Thebes. The lions before mentioned formerly stretched into the centre of the walk, from pillar to pillar, but are now removed, and placed on each side, in a line with the rest, so that an uninterrupted view is now had of the entire length of the gallery and its saloons. The large Head of Ramesses II, and its companion, stand in the centre saloon, and form striking objects as the visitor passes between them into the Phygalian Saloon.

The walls of the building have been coloured in dull red; the ceiling is in compartments, with sunk panels, the ground of which is painted blue, with a Grecian ornament in gold; the mouldings around are in red and gold. The moulding under the windows and above the newly arranged shelves is gilded and painted. The whole effect is very pleasing.

## The Egyptian Room at the British Museum
*Illustrated London News,* February 13, 1847

Our illustration shows one of the new rooms in the upper floor of the western wing of our national museum — the Egyptian Room, the first apartment to the right of the Great Staircase leading to the Ethnographical Room. It has cases ranged on either side, filled with Egyptian deities, sacred animals, statues, household furniture, and other large objects. But here, as everywhere else, last of all comes death; and the floor of the room is mostly occupied with plate glass cases of mummies, and various emblems of the painted pageantry to which mortals have fondly clung in all ages of the world. Here are coffins, sepulchral cones, and other ornaments, scaraboei, amulets etc. The casts illustrate the heroic life of Egypt, just as the contents of the cases illustrate the social life. This room has usually crowds of visitors; and, when we remember that Egypt was the cradle of civilisation, we shall not be surprised at its relics being so popular.

### The Museum of Sir John Soane
*Illustrated London News,* June 25, 1864

June is one of the three months of the London season in which this treasure-house of art can be most fully visited by the public; on which account, as well as on that of the growing interest of the Museum, the present time may be considered most opportune for its illustration. One of our views represents the sepulchral chamber, in the lower part of the museum, which contains the splendid ancient Egyptian sarcophagus, discovered by Belzoni in 1817 in a royal tomb in the valley of Biban el Malook, near Gournou, Thebes. It was bought by Sir John Soane of Mr. Salt, the traveller, in 1824, for the sum of £ 2,000.

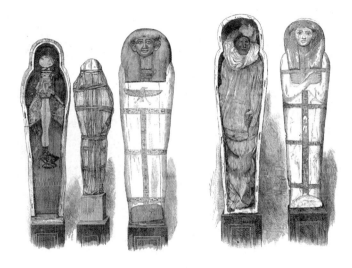

# Archaeology

### Cleopatra's Needle, Alexandria, Presented to England by Mohammed Ali Pasha, Being Examined by Sir James Alexander
The *Graphic*, November 20, 1875

To commemorate the services rendered to Egypt by the Battle of Aboukir, won by Nelson in 1798, and the Battle of Alexandria, where Abercromby fell in 1801, Mohammed Ali, who was then Pasha of Egypt, offered to our nation three notable relics of antiquity, namely, an obelisk at Luxor, the great statue of Sesostris at Memphis, and one of Cleopatra's needles, which had been lying for ages prostrate in the sand, thirty feet only from the sea-wall of Alexandria, and close to the scene of Abercromby's action. An Earthquake is supposed to have thrown it down. Up to the present time, our gifts have remained unremoved. To move the two first would probably be a costly operation, but Cleopatra's needle lies, as has already been stated, close to the waterside, and the French did not grudge £80,000 — to move a twin obelisk from Luxor to the Place de la Concorde in Paris.

When Major-General Sir James Alexander was in Paris in 1867, and as an antiquary was admiring the obelisk, he heard that a Frenchman, owner of the ground where the British obelisk lies, intended to break it up, as we did not seem to care for it, and it was in his way of projected buildings. For seven years the General vainly strove to induce the Government to move it to London. Objectors said that the obelisk had been so long unclaimed, the Khedive might object to its removal, and might desire to set it up along with the upright obelisk in the great square of Alexandria; that there was a building on it — a part of the fortifications; and lastly, that it was mutilated, and not worth removing.

To set the matter at rest, General Alexander visited Egypt in the spring of this year at his own expense. He found that the Khedive ruled no objection to the removal of the obelisk, that there was no building on it, and that it was in excellent preservation; in far better condition than its upright sister, the hieroglyphs on two sides of which have been abraded by the wind and sand of the desert for centuries. Having obtained permission from M. Dimitri, a highly-respectable and wealthy Greek gentleman, the present proprietor of the ground, General Alexander spent three weeks at and about the obelisk, which he found lying in a shallow trench near its upright companion. With the assistance of Mr. Wynman Dixon, of the North of England Iron Company, he took three feet of sand off it. The obelisk, on being uncovered, was found to be 68 feet long, a noble mass of syenite, or rose-coloured granite. The upper face was then washed by means of the water-skin of an Egyptian water-carrier, and the hieroglyphics came well out on it. These were then translated by Brugsch Bey, a well known Egyptologist. Thotmes II had caused the obelisk to be prepared 1,600 B.C., or 3,475 years ago. The central column of hieroglyphics are for Thotmes, the latest columns are for Ramesses III, and recount his life and achievements. The obelisk is now totally uncovered and photographed. The hieroglyphics are on four sides, and are well preserved by the sand about them, and, as the weight is under 200 tons, it is quite moveable by skilled hands. Its height above the sea is fifteen feet. The plans and papers regarding it are in Mr. Disraeli's hands. A fine site has been allocated it by the Metropolitan Board of Works on the Thames Embankment, and it is earnestly hoped that funds may be forthcoming for bringing it to this country.

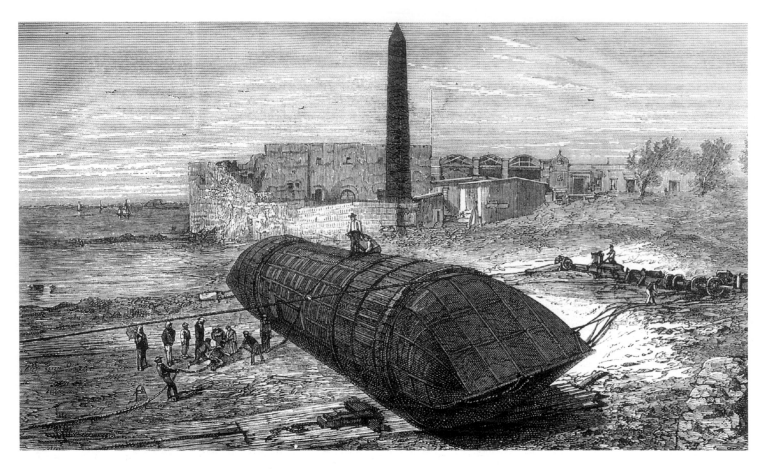

## Cleopatra's Needle: An Illustrated History of the Obelisk Belonging to Great Britain, and of other Egyptian Monoliths
The *Graphic*, February 2, 1878

On September 15th we illustrated the launch from the beach, and additional illustrations are given in the present number, as well as one showing how the iron cocoon was deftly woven piecemeal round the chrysalis within, and another of the packing of the Needle in its case. So vigorously had the works been pushed forward that the cylinder was rolled down the beach on the 28th of August, but owing to the piercing of its skin by a sunken rock at about the last ten or twenty yards of the hundred it had to traverse, it did not get into deep water until the 7th of September. But for this mishap, and allowing for the fortnight spent in transforming the cylindroid into a ship in the Khedive's dry dock, nine miles from the old Roman port and the Cæsarium, and for other necessary preliminaries, the final start for England would not have been delayed until the ominous equinoctial Friday, the 21st.

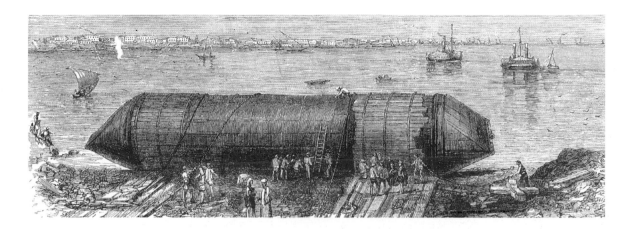

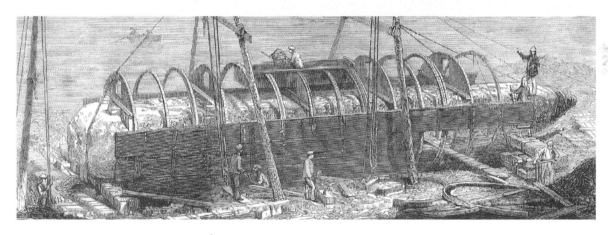

## Abandonment of Cleopatra's Needle in the Bay of Biscay
*Illustrated London News*
October 27, 1877

The south-west gale of Sunday, the fourteenth, raging in the Bay of Biscay, as well as in England, compelled the abandonment, early next morning, of Mr. Dixon's ingenious vessel, or iron-plate cylinder, named the *Cleopatra*, in which the Egyptian obelisk from Alexandria was being towed by the steamer *Olga* on its voyage to London… The *Cleopatra* was afterwards picked up by a steamer bound for the Spanish port of Valencia; and we have since learned that the obelisk, in its still floating iron case, is left in safety at Ferrol, whence it will no doubt be brought to its destination.

### The Machinery for Placing the Obelisk in Position on the Thames Embankment
*The Graphic*, June 1, 1878

The difficulties which Mr. Dixon has had to contend with in order to carry out his work in connection with the transport of the Egyptian obelisk to England having at last been overcome, the concluding and most difficult part of the undertaking, that of raising and placing the obelisk on its pedestal is about to be commenced. A timber cradle has been prepared alongside the Adelphi steps, and by the time this paper is published the *Cleopatra* will probably be safely landed upon it; she is then to be lifted by hydraulic jacks and moved forward at the same time, and afterwards a little sideways, until the stone lies across the centre of its pedestal. The iron cylinder vessel, in which the voyage was made, will then be cut to pieces and twenty feet in length of the centre part of the obelisk will be encased in an iron jacket with protruding arms, resembling the trunnions of a monster cannon. These trunnions will rest on two iron girder. A timber scaffolding will then be erected with for uprights, each formed of six baulks of timber placed three and three together, the ends of the girders fitting into the spaces between the timbers. Hydraulic jacks will then be placed underneath the girders, and the whole mass gradually lifted, the height gained being secured by solid timber packing. The stone will then exactly represent a monster cannon, and can be swung on its trunnions into a vertical position, and lowered on to its pedestal, which meantime will have been constructed beneath it. Our illustration is drawn from the model to which Mr. Dixon's men are working.

### The Egyptian Sphinx
*Illustrated London News*, June 19, 1886

Our illustration shows the present state of the excavations now being carried on for the purpose of clearing away the sand around the Great Sphinx at Giza, near Cairo. M. Maspero the present eminent Director-in-Chief of the Boulak Museum at Cairo, having obtained a grant of £8,000, which sum has been augmented by another £1,000, contributed from private sources, commenced this work two or three months ago; and he is to be congratulated on the great progress it has made. The sand has been quite cleared away form the large tablet, bearing an inscription in hieroglyphic writing, placed on the bosom of the Sphinx; the paws, and the passage between them have been freed from sand; and the small altar, supposed to have been used by the Romans for sacrificial purposes, is now exposed to view. Those persons who have only seen the Sphinx buried to the shoulders in sand, and gazing with mystic and solemn mien over the silent desert, can form but little conception of its present appearance, standing high in the air, and surrounded by crowds of children of both sexes, carrying baskets of sand, which are removed by tram-rail wagons, and by the usual nineteenth century appliances for such a work.

The Sphinx, which is near the three great Pyramids at Giza, seven or eight miles from Cairo, on the western or Libyan bank of the Nile, is well known to every tourist in Egypt. It is a recumbent figure, with the body of a beast, supposed to be that of a lion, and with a male human head. The body, which is 140 feet long, and the lower part of the head, are mainly cut out of the natural rock, but some parts are filled in with stone masonry; the head is 14 feet wide, and was formerly capped with a head-dress, which is destroyed, but the shape of which is represented in sculptured tablets showing this figure. Its builder and designer, and the date of its formation are not certainly determined; it is one of the oldest monuments in Egypt. It is thought to have belonged to a vast series of temples, which existed before the Great Pyramid was erected by Shoo-foo, *Cheops*, one of the Kings of the Fourth Dynasty; and to have stood between the Temple of Isis and that of Osiris. It was called the Image of *Hor-em-khoo*, which means, "the sun at rest," and may have had an astro-

nomical, as well as a mythological and a symbolical or mystical significance. Excavations at its base were commenced in 1817 by Caviglia, who found there some tablets deposited by later kings of Egypt. The late Mariette Bey, Director of the Government Museum of Antiquities, resumed this work; but much sand has since been suffered to accumulate.

## The Discoveries at the Brick Pyramids of Dahchour, near Memphis
The *Graphic*, May 26, 1894

Until recently, the two brick pyramids of Dahchour might have been included among the monuments which were full of mystery, and which had hitherto not enriched the stores of nineteenth century knowledge. These pyramids are called by the Arabs the "black pyramids," and they have excited the curiosity of travellers from the time of Herodotus, who said of them that they were even more mysterious than their sisters the stone pyramids. At one time these brick pyramids had an outer covering of stone, but this was taken away by a well-known Egyptian conqueror, the famous Sesostris, who did not hesitate to denude these pyramids of their carved stone facings so as to enrich and enlarge the beautiful temple of Ptah at Memphis. Today the pyramids are little better than shapeless mounds, although a close inspection shows how well each pile had originally been constructed, and of what good material it had been composed, to stand so long after being deprived of its protecting stone covering.

So early as the year 1839, Mr. Perring, who had been sent out on behalf of the British Museum, had attempted to cut his way into the more northerly of the two brick pyramids, but without result. The Egyptian Government department which concerns itself with the discovery and preservation of Egyptian antiquities, a department founded by the French *savant* M. Mariette, the discoverer of many of the Memphis remains, has made several attempts to probe the depths of the mystery of the "black pyramids," and in 1881, under the direction of M. Maspero, an excavation on an unusually large scale was commenced on the north side of the larger pyramid. It was expected that the secret entrance to the innermost chambers would soon be reached. The work was continued for two years and was then given up.

The new director of the department, M. de Morgan, being satisfied that the efforts of his predecessors had not been properly directed, determined to make a fresh attack on this mysterious and impregnable fortress of the dead. So in February this year he established himself in Dahchour, and shortly after his arrival some hundreds of *fellahs* were engaged to make excavations. The men dug the sand and filled the baskets for the women and children to carry off, the whole crowd singing all day long their peculiar songs, of which the words vary but seldom and the tune never. M. de

Morgan commenced by excavating the tombs situated round the pyramid, by which he was enabled to make researches proving the period to which the tombs, as well as the pyramids, belonged. These tombs were the burial places of the richest of the inhabitants of Memphis who lived in the reigns of the Kings who built the pyramids; the better class of people, and the courtiers, being able to afford to be buried close to the burial place of the Kings. About thirty mastabas, as these tombs are called, were laid bare, among them being the sepulchers of several grand court functionaries. All the tombs were built on the same simple principle, each being covered by a mass of stone masonry ornamented on the sides with sculptured funereal figures, while in each case the entrance to the tomb was from the north, whence a passage led to a pit more or less deep in which the sarcophagus had been deposited. This was, of course, the mode of burial in vogue up to and including the Twelfth Dynasty.

As a result of his researches M. de Morgan was able to prove that the large pyramid was built on a plan similar to the small tombs, for he set his men to dig carefully all along the northern base of the pyramid inside the outer surrounding wall, until one day his enterprise and patience were rewarded by the discovery of an entrance to a pit in which was an opening leading to a tortuous narrow passage. At the end of this passage was a tomb with a rifled sarcophagus–rifled by the spoliators of a bygone age, perhaps in the time of the Romans. This sarcophagus chamber led to a gallery about 120 yards long. The pit by which entry had thus been obtained into the pyramid was evidently not the true and original entrance, but a pit made by the people who had

rifled the tomb of its treasure. The difficulty now was to find the proper doorway. And this was all the more necessary since it was found impossible to remain inside the gallery without being suffocated, and an opening near the other end of this gallery would establish some ventilation which would enable the workers to carry on their explorations. At length the proper entrance was found. It led to twelve vaults more or less spacious, of which the contents—sarcophagi, offerings, canopies, carpets, etc.,—had been stolen or rifled at some remote period of antiquity. Most of the objects left behind contained no inscriptions; but the few hieroglyphics remaining showed that the explorers were in the burial-place of a family of high estate; in fact of a whole series of princesses, and among them actually the coffin of the Queen Nofert-Hout, and the coffin of the royal daughter Ment-Sent-Senbetes.

But the discovery that placed the date of these burials as having taken place in the middle of the medium or middle Empire,

during the time of the most powerful dynasty of that period, was made a few days later. M. de Morgan was carefully clearing the floor of the passage when he discovered, under the spade of one of his assistants, a hiding place scarcely covered by the sand, and which had not been noticed by those robbers of bygone days. In this secret receptacle was a little wooden box, quite rotten, filled with jewels of perfectly marvellous workmanship. This box was carefully conveyed to the museum at Giza. The principal jewel was a breastpiece of gold, encrusted with precious stones of remarkable beauty and of very fine workmanship. On this was depicted two eagles guarding the tomb

carried on. This pyramid is not nearly in so good a state of preservation as the northern one. Here the work was commenced on the 6th of the last month, and a series of excavations have been made along the north side, as in the case of the previous pyramid. Some of the discoveries already made will be of great scientific value. The first was the tomb of a king whose name has hitherto been unknown in the compiled lists of Egyptian monarchs. This king's name is Hor Rafou-ab, and his place is at the end of the Twelfth Dynasty. The tomb also contained a wooden coffin, covered with bands of gold engraved with hieroglyph-ics, and a statue made of

of Osirtasen II. The rest of the jewellery consisted of necklaces, bracelets, and scores of various little trinkets.

The following day the explorers brought to light, close to the sarcophagus of another princess, a still larger box of jewels, of which the principal were two breastplates, on which are inscribed the names of Osirtasen III and Amenemha, while around the names the enemies of these two kings are depicted being thrown to the ground.

Encouraged by these finds, the explorers continued their researches, but as yet the vault, containing the mummy of the king for whom the pyramid was constructed, has not been discovered. Success will, however, crown M. de Morgan's efforts, which have been delayed by the mass of débris caused by the former excava-tors.

In the meantime, at the other brick pyramid, situated nearly two miles to the south of the first, some important work was being

acacia wood, and representing the king. This coffin stood close by and is ornamented similarly to the real coffin. Hieroglyphics cover the gold bands. The statue, which is almost life-size, represents a young man of extraordinary beauty, and is a wonderful example of Egyptian art; in fact, it throws quite a new light on the art of the period.

The next vault had been left intact, and was found just as the mourners left it thousands of years ago, with the funeral offerings surrounding the sarcophagus. A princess had been buried here. Her name was Noub-Hotep, and in then were enclosed jewels of great interest. A scourge was also in the coffin.

This is how matters stand in Dahchour. The two pyramids have not altogether disclosed their secrets, but M. de Morgan is quite justified in expecting that success will crown his well-directed labours. The value of these latest researches can, of course, hardly be estimated as yet.

# Part Two

# Daily Life
*People, Places & Events*

The pharaonic past was not the only subject of interest in Egypt for the Victorians. The phantasmagoria of Egypt's present was a source of equal if not surpassing fascination, and received due reflection in the mirror of the press. Through sets of illustrations that appeared for several consecutive weeks under such titles as *Egypt as It Is*, or *Life in Egypt*, the papers sought to categorize the ethnographic diversity that existed in both urban and rural landscapes and to create a typology at once humdrum and exotic. In this attempt they complemented the great works compiled earlier in the century such as the *Description de l'Egypte* and *Manners and Customs of the Modern Egyptians*, but made their observations on even the most esoteric subjects available and familiar to a far wider audience. Though this audience may have been contemptuous at times and often patronizing, if the tone of the coverage was an adequate reflection of the outlook of the reader, it was undoubtedly well-informed. All the wealth of descriptive detail collected in the newspapers contributed to an imposing panorama of the quotidian.

It was not merely the people of Egypt that were objects of curiosity: their habitat was also subject to close scrutiny. What had largely been a generic imaginative geography of the Orient began to reveal specificities. Within the topography of Cairo, modernity could be seen beside a significantly unchanged mediaeval heritage. The labyrinthine complexity of the old Arab city, with its fertile sites for the imagination such as the slave market and the bazaar, provided a metaphor for the deviousness of the oriental mind. But both locations had their parallels in the European city. The macabre fascination of the slave market, in which the living body became a commodity, could be matched by the attraction of the Parisian morgue, where the dead body was put on public view. The bazaar — the original locus of the world in miniature where all things could be bought and sold — was the forerunner of the arcades to be found in urban developments throughout nineteenth century Europe. Cairo's Old City provided a stark contrast to the newest quarters of town with their fake Saracenic buildings designed by foreign architects and their axially-directed thoroughfares that sliced through the chaos of ancient and tortuous alleyways. The new buildings provided romance without dirt, while the new roads were eminently suitable as routes for both sewers and soldiers.

The newspapers' correspondents also provided documentation of important contemporary events and festive occasions. The visits of royalty, and in particular that of the Prince and Princess of Wales, generated a good deal of publicity. Colourful annual customs, such as the Mahmal procession, the Doseh, and the Gebr al-Khalig must have fulfilled all expectations of oriental mystery. Less mysterious, but no less colourful were imported social gatherings such as the race-meetings. Illustrations of these entertainments appeared alongside renderings of routine tragedies — the bread and butter of the journalist — here represented in a manner so picturesque as to mislead the viewer almost entirely about the true nature of the subject-matter.

# People

## Musicians of the Sudan at an Arab Coffee House in Old Cairo
*Illustrated London News*
April 21, 1883

The Arabs, like most of the oriental nations, are passionately fond of music; and some of the favourite performers in the streets and the court-yards of large houses are natives of the Sudan, whose wild, sweet, irregular strains of melody, produced by the aid of a rudely constructed lyre with five strings and a flute or whistle made of reed, accompanied by the beating of a drum, are not unpleasing even to a culti-vated ear. Many of the performers sing what are supposed to be extempore dit-ties, but those who understand the lan-guage report that these songs are full of lascivious and indecent jokes. These are attended with a good deal of action, ges-ture, and grimace, which seem to afford much amusement to the Arabs and low-class Egyptians; but few European spec-tators would care to watch them more than a few minutes.

## Sketches in Egypt: Courtyard of a House at Cairo
*Illustrated London News,* March 10, 1883

Our Artist who was not long since employed in delineating the picturesque features of native Egyptian life and manners, with the ordinary aspects of Cairo and the other Mohammedan towns of that interesting land of the Nile, furnishes the sketch of a party assembled to witness the performance of snake-charmers, in the courtyard of a large house in the city. This is a scene peculiarly characteristic of the popular taste for marvellous and amusing entertainments; and the domestic architecture of Cairo, as well as the costume of the people, is very faithfully represented by our Artist in this genuine illustration of their common social life. The exhibition of tame serpents, which are perfectly harmless, and which show much docility under instruction, while their movements are singularly graceful and beautiful, has always been a favourite pastime of the Eastern nations.

## A Barber's Shop at Cairo
*Illustrated London News*
January 28, 1893

Life in Egypt, at least in the city of Cairo, presents the strangest jumble of Mohammedan and European and Levantine characteristics, in habits, manners, and customs, often described in books and letters, yet not easily imagined. The barber's shop which appears on our front page is one of the trivial incidents that meet the eye of an amused English tourist.

**The People of Egypt**
*Illustrated London News*, September 30, 1882

1) Instead of a Latch-key  2) Janissary of the Greek Consulate
3) Cleaning Wool  4) A Public Letter Writer  5) Janissary of the
British Consulate

**The People of Egypt**
*Illustrated London News*, September 30, 1882

1) Arab Shoeblacks in Alexandria  2) Night Watchman  3) Water-
Carrier  4) Street Barber  5) Liquorice-Water Seller  6) Seller of Water
7) Street Coffee-Seller  8) Seller of Sweetmeats  9) Porter

## A Marriage in Cairo
*Illustrated London News,* November 20, 1897
(Text from *ILN,* November 18, 1882)

Our Artist has made a sketch of a Mussulman wedding in Cairo. The condition of women in Egypt is said to be rather more favourable than in Turkey; and polygamy, though a legal institution, is not practiced in one family out of twenty, among the middle class and the labouring class of the population. The worst abuse of the Mohammedan law matrimonial is the facility of divorce by the husband, almost at his own caprice; but the divorced wife is entitled to a separate maintenance, for a certain period, at her husband's cost, and the custody of her children until the age of seven years. Egyptian girls can be married at ten years of age, and many become mothers at fourteen. The wives are very industrious and careful housekeepers, while those of the richer class bestow much time on fine needlework and embroidery, enjoy singing and dancing, and meet their female gossips in lengthy visits and social parties, from which the men are strictly excluded. The peasant women commonly go unveiled, and have as much freedom, with as kind treatment, as the wives of poor working men in any Christian country.

## Howling Dervishes in Old Cairo
*Illustrated London News*, October 21, 1882

Old Cairo, or *El Fustat*, three miles south of the existing chief city, is mostly in ruins; it was built after the Arab conquest of Egypt, A.D. 641, on the site of a Roman military town, the remains of which are still to be seen. Villas with gardens are here pleasantly situated near the banks of the river, and there is a Greek convent, a church on the supposed ground where Joseph and Mary rested after their flight into Egypt; and the dilapidated, but formerly magnificent, Mosque of Amrou, with its 200 columns of granite, porphyry, and marble. The performances of the dancing and howling dervishes, who constitute the Salvation Army of Mohammedan religious enthusiasm, may be witnessed every Friday in their stated places of assembly; they form a curious exhibition of fantastic gestures, which our artist has represented in his sketch.

## Ploughing in Lower Egypt
*Illustrated London News,* August 19, 1876

The picture engraved represents a class of subject far more frequently treated by the painter of oriental life. The scene is one on the special beauty of which the traveller has often expatiated. The refreshed and gladdened earth smiles under a serene blue sky; across which float only a few waifs of golden morning cloud; for the great and marvellous phenomenon of the periodical inundation of the Nile valley, to which alone the country owes its prosperity from time immemorial, has come and gone. It is time for the *fellaheen* to speed the plough, to hoe and to sow, as

we see them here. But where else could one find so primitive a plough, or so strange a yoke? Probably the plough is of the same form as in the days of the pharaohs, if not, indeed, of still ruder construction. The *fellah* has to procure animals of draught whence he may. The Egyptian oxen, which have something of the character of the bison or buffalo, are sturdy beasts; but they are not plentiful. So the patient camel, with all the gear for his being ridden, is also put to the plough. They are an ill-assorted pair; it may not be easy to drive and direct them; yet they appear to work tolerably well together.

# Places

**The Slave Market, Cairo**
The *Graphic*, October 7, 1882

Cairo, in spite of the fact that under the reforming Khedive Ismail it was largely *Haussmannized*, is still an Oriental city. Our engraving gives us a glimpse of one of the baser sides of Oriental life. Domestic slavery—the slavery of the harem—still flourishes vigorously in the Egyptian capital. On this point, the use and wont of centuries, and the deeply ingrained belief of the Mohammedan that divine prerogative entitles him to three, four, or more wives (if he can afford to keep them), has successfully contended against the anti-slavery proposals of European diplomatists. Nubian, Circassian, and Abyssinian women are still in great demand, though representations from the West have done something to suppress sales in open market. As will be seen from our engraving, the old slave market is now in an almost ruinous state.

## A Street in Cairo–the Gourieh
*Illustrated London News*, September 24, 1881

The famous capital city of Mohammedan Egypt has been considerably Frenchified in some parts by the intrusion of European tastes and fashions. The oldest and still most characteristic quarter is that which occupies the site of the town built in the twelfth century of the Christian era, by the Caliphs of the Fatimeh line, with the extension of the city southward toward the base of Mount Mukattam, where the citadel was erected by their successor Saladin. This runs along the whole eastern side of Cairo, and is divided longitudinally from north to south by a series of high streets or principal thoroughfares, called in different parts the *Souk en Nahasin*, or coppersmiths' bazaar, the *Gourieh*, and the *Soukariyeh*, or sugar market. Many by-streets diverge from these main thoroughfares, especially to the east, branching off into a great number of crooked alleys and closed courts, which are the separate resorts of different trades, or else the secluded habitations of private families. Most of these were formerly guarded by ponderous wooden gates, which at night were shut and barred by a porter, but now this is seldom done. There is commonly a shop on the ground floor of each house, but it is quite separate from the dwellings in the upper apartments, and takes but little of the space in the building. It is merely a recess, about 6 feet high, and only 4 feet broad, with a few shelves, and with a stone seat, perhaps, upon which the shopkeeper may sit, smoke and gossip, and discuss a bargain. In front of the stall hangs a shutter, which he lets down at night, and fastens with a padlock, when it is time for him to go home, or when he visits the mosque, bath or the coffeehouse. Many shops of the same trade, in a bazaar of that trade, stand side by side, and on both sides of the narrow lane. The long main thoroughfare, from the *Bab el Futteh*, or north-east city gate, to near the citadel at the opposite end, passes through a series of bazaars, those of the smiths, the miscellaneous dealers, the sellers of dried fruit, the vendors of sugar and sweetmeats, and the shoemakers. All the other trades have their special bazaars, to the right hand or the left. On the east side is a collection of streets known as the *Gemaliyeh*, where the native wholesale merchants have their business establishments; and the *Khan el Khalily*, the chief depot of the Red Sea trade. Further on are the stalls of the booksellers, the market for goods from the Sudan, and the street of the armourers, which was formerly renowned for its fine display of sword blades, and of sword hilts and pistols, often mounted with gold or silver, richly chased and jewelled. On the other side of the main thoroughfare is the *Margush,* or cotton-market; again the intricate labyrinth of streets just wide enough to walk through, occupied by the silversmiths and the jewellers. Farther back is the *Hamzawy,* or Christians' market for the sale of European goods, and the *Musky,* or Jewish quarter.

## Rue de l'Hôtel Shepheard & the Palace of Gezeereh
The *Graphic*, September 30, 1882

There may be transit-passengers through Egypt of a some-what illiterate type, who take no interest in the Sphinx or the Pyramids, but they have probably all heard of Shepheard's Hotel. It is situated on one side of the Esbekieh: a sort of Cairene Champs Elysee. The street by which Shepheard, the founder of this popular *caravanserai*, has thus become immortalised, runs from the Place de l'Opera to the Alexandria Railway Station on the other side of the Ismailia Canal.

There is no old palace at Cairo: all are of modern date. That of Gezeereh was built by the Khedive Ismail, and is situated on the left bank of the river opposite Boulak, the road from the city leading across the iron bridge of Kasr en Nil. The outside presents no remarkable feature, except some handsome ironwork. The entrance hall and staircase are very fine, and the reception rooms are magnificently decorated, many of the articles of furniture being beautiful works of art. The gardens are (or *were* till lately) carefully kept up. In them is a very pretty kiosk after the style of the Alhambra.

## Interior of the Mosque of El-Azhar, Cairo
*Illustrated London News,* May 2, 1896

Native religious preachers, mollahs, and ulemas: all these ecclesiastics, and a clergy without a priesthood make up no small part of social life in "Egypt As It Is." Religion is extremely popular in that country; while the el-Azhar, the great Theological College of Cairo, with its three hundred learned professors of divinity and law, according to the Koran and Arabic Commentaries upon it, is frequented by students from all parts of the East. We may here recommend, to those of our readers who care to know more of the Mohammedan doctrine, the newest little volume of Messrs. Macmillan's "Golden Treasury" series; which is *The Speeches and Table-Talk of the prophet Mohammed*, selected and translated by Mr. Stanley Lane-Poole, and Arabic scholar of hereditary repute.

# Events

**The Races at Cairo: Canter in Front of the Grand Stand Before the Start**
*Illustrated London News*, February 6, 1864

The Cairo Races established by the present Viceroy were run for the first time on the 5th ult. [of last month], on the desert near Abbasieh, distant about three miles from the city. The course was an oval of two miles in length by half a mile in width; the ground was hard sand mixed with pebbles, and was broken by transverse ruts formed by the rain - on the whole, tolerable good ground and not too deep. The first race was for Arab horses, three miles for £ 500 and £ 100 to the second; it was won by *Hamdany*, belonging to Mr. Smart, after a close contest with *Dukhy*, owned by Halim Pasha. The second race, for horses of all nations, catch

weights, was five miles for £ 300, and £ 100 to the second. Four English horses ran, but were beaten without a struggle by an Arab horse of the Obeyan breed, who, however, lost the race by his rider dismounting at the third mile, which permitted a chestnut mare of Ali Pasha's to come in first, the Obeyan recovering the second place. The third race was for £ 100, two miles, and was gained by Ali Pasha after a close race with a grey mare belonging to M. Guichard, but not well ridden. Altogether it was a great success.

A kiosk was erected for the Viceroy, and a grand-stand for the Europeans. A buffet was provided of twenty-five tables, each of six covers, besides the private table for his Highness and his guests, all at the Viceroy's expense. The course was properly staked and corded, and kept by cavalry pickets and mounted police, and the whole passed off without any quarrel or accident of any kind. Two fine regimental bands performed in the intervals between the courses. At the conclusion of the day, a purse of £ 100 was run for by the Bashi-Bazouk cavalry, who dashed off in a dense clump, forming a very pretty and animating spectacle. Mr. Smart, of Alexandria, was intrusted by the Viceroy with all the arrangements; and it is to his exertions, aided by the Viceroy's liberality, that the great success attending this attempt to introduce racing into Egypt must be attributed.

## The Doseh
*Illustrated London News,* November 30, 1861

This most remarkable of the many peculiar ceremonies in connection with the Moslem religion takes place on the last day of the festival of the birthday of the Prophet. The *fête* is held in a portion of the gardens of the Esbekieh in Cairo, and lasts nine days. Though it has lost something in repute it is still tolerably well attended, and by the very orthodox much venerated. A great number of marquees are erected, which are brilliantly illuminated at night with innumerable glass lamps. These places are used by dervishes and others for the performance of the *zikkr*—a religious and somewhat laborious exercise, producing a species of hysteria, called *milboos* by the Arabs. There are also other amusements of a more attractive kind, such as dancing-men, conjurors, and storytellers.

On the ninth and last day of the fête the chief Sheik of the *Saadeyeh*, or Dervishes, at an early hour starts from the mosque al-Hassaneyn, where, it is said, he has spent the previous night in prayer and fasting, and proceeds to the house of the *Sheik al-Bekru* (or chief priest). On the route the procession is joined by numbers of dervishes, from the various districts of the metropolis, with their distinguishing flags. The march is further enlivened by several individuals who execute voluntaries on reed pipes, with independent variations on drums. A herd of men walking four or five abreast precede the Sheik. They are the devotees who are about to undergo the ordeal of the Doseh, arm-in-arm and rolling their heads from side to side, uttering a hoarse cry of "allahhu!" continually, apparently lost to everything but paradise and eternity. The great excitement under which they appear to be labouring is unnatural, and would require stronger stimulants than any religious exercise could afford.

Following this mixed mob of fanatics, dervishes, flags, drums, and soldiers, is the Sheik himself on horseback, escorted by a detachment of grenadiers from the viceregal guard and a crowd of officious ecclesiastics. On their arrival at the south end of the Esbekieh, and opposite to the house of the Sheik al-Bekru, the devotees, urged by the dervishes, throw themselves flat upon the ground and are then carefully arranged and packed (care being taken to have the heads all one way), and continue their cry of "*Allah!*" which is taken up by the spectators, who become very much excited. The Sheik's horse is of powerful build, highly trained, and unshod, but always hesitates to place its foot on the first body: this difficulty, however, being gotten over by the aid of some gentle inducements administered by the attendant priests, he ambles freely, but with singular care, over the whole; each man is trodden upon twice.  It is rarely, if ever, that the horse misses his footing—placing one foot on the shoulder of one man and one hind foot upon the hip of another. Immediately the sheik has passed over, the men leap up, shouting the usual "*Allahhu!*" The excitement at this particular moment is intense, and the *cawasses,* police, are extremely lively and energetic in keeping the mob back. Amongst the crowd may be observed some of the fanatics termed *saadeyeh,* almost in a state of nudity: they profess to eat glass and snakes besides other vermin. Others of the same sect, who generally accompany or are present at religious festivals and processions, appear to pass iron pins of about one foot in length, surmounted with a heavy ball of the same metal, through their faces and other parts of the body, even throwing them into the air and receiving them point downward in their eyes, which they appear to penetrate some two or three inches. No marks are visible upon their withdrawal; in fact, the performances of these worthy gentlemen are highly creditable, and would undoubtedly earn them a decent livelihood in the streets of London.

The Doseh, like many other Moslem observances, has not escaped the hand of innovation, and even now shows marked symptoms of decay.  The number of devotees who present themselves to be operated upon have greatly decreased within the last few years, and they are of the lowest orders. The spectators are equally affected, and, with the exception of a few cases, are generally indifferent. Even the astounding performances of the dervishes scarcely provoke more than the usual exclamation of "*Mashallah!*" (Praise be to God).

## The Festival of Gebr-el-Haleeg, or Breaking the Canal
*Illustrated London News*, November 1, 1862

This very ancient and singular festival takes place annually in the neighbourhood of Cairo, and, as its name implies, is simply the breaking or cutting of a dam that is constructed at the mouth of the Cairo Canal after the Nile has commenced rising, which generally happens about the period of the summer solstice. In the space between the dam and the river a cone of mud, is raised. This rude attempt at an effigy is called the *Aroosah* or bride; and, to complete the delusion, some Indian corn is sown upon the top. This figure is washed down by the river when it reaches a certain height. It is supposed to have been substituted for a human being who was formerly sacrificed every year by the ancient Egyptians, a practice which we are told by Arab historians was abolished after the conquest of Egypt by the followers of Mohammed. The traditions have it that the ancients entertained such a profound veneration for their beautiful Nile, and understood so well how much they were indebted to it as the sole source of their wealth and power, that, in order to testify their gratitude for past services, and by way of a gentle hint that a continuance of those favours would not be objected to, it was their custom every year, at a certain season and at a particular spot, to immolate a young virgin by drowning. This agreeable process was supposed to ensure an abundant overflow. Although this barbarious custom was prohibited, the festival has been always observed, like others of a superstitious nature common to the Greeks which have been retained and participated in by the Moslems, the festival in question having more of a political than religious character about it. Europeans and natives freely mix together on this occasion.

The accompanying illustration represents a scene on a portion of the River Nile, near the mouth of the Cairo Canal, as it appeared on the night of the *Yôm Wefa el Nil* (or "day of the completion or abundance of the river,") occurring this year on the 13th of August. The amusements are continued throughout the night, and at an early hour on the following morning the water is admitted into the canal. As the religious prejudices and antagonisms of creed are not called into play, every one who can manage it makes this festival the occasion of a little excusable dissipation. Those who can afford it prefer passing the evening on board a *dahabieh*, or pleasure-boat, with their families; and, indeed, this is the only comfortable way of

enjoying the thing, provided the boat is tolerably free from crawl-
ing vermin and the commissariat properly organised.

A night on the Nile in one of those luxurious *dahabieh* is agreeable at any season, but particularly so during the hot months, from
June to September. Within this period the thermometer averages
from 98 degrees to 104 degrees in the shade from 10 a.m. to 4 p.m.
A Cairene is therefore living almost in the atmosphere of a Turkish
bath, and is but too glad to drag his attenuated and debilitated
form to some secluded spot (after sunset) and inhale the fresh
evening breeze, and feast his eyes upon the overflowing Nile and

its picturesque shores. The sketch can convey but a very feeble idea
of a scene so bustling and picturesque, as all who have witnessed
the festival will readily allow. Shortly after sunset the fireworks
commence, and continue at intervals throughout the night. On this
occasion the display was more than ordinarily magnificent. The
government, with a laudable desire to please and to amuse, was
actually prodigal in this respect. A battery of fieldpieces in position
upon the plain, in the immediate vicinity of the canal, varied the
entertainments by occasional salvos, the natives having the keenest
relish for this description of music. It is quite delightful to observe

the intense enjoyment of the crowds of eager, open-mouthed, many-coloured people who line the shore, and who are packed so tight that if any one of them ventured upon a sneeze a perceptible tremor would be observed over the whole concourse. Notwithstanding the heat, inconvenience, and fatigue of remaining so many hours in the same place and position, the people bear their sufferings with the most exemplary fortitude. Those of the unwashed, who, being late, have to put up with a position in the extreme rear, which just commands a limited view of a few turbans in the immediate neighbourhood or a stray rocket now and then high above their heads—even these excellent characters are satisfied, and return to their homes and labours rejoicing "*Mashallah!*"

On the water, in a comfortable boat, things are much more agreeable. In order to command a good view of the scene the boats are anchored as near as possible to the island of Rhoda. This small island is situated opposite Old Cairo, and is celebrated for its Nilometer. Having taken up a good position, the spectator has leisure to make his observations with a certain degree of comfort. The noise and confusion are astounding. Steamers and sailing-vessels are crowded together promiscuously; all are decorated with variegated lamps, and most have some kind of amusement on board. Two or three bands in close proximity to each other are indefatigable in their efforts to make themselves heard. The discord is frightful, let alone the eternal banging of drums and pattering of *darabookahs* (a small drum played by the hands).

An occasional peep into the cabins of the *dahabiehs* as they slowly drift past reveals picturesque groups of singing-girls, in gay and fanciful costumes. Many of these girls are good looking, and mostly possess remarkably clear and soft voices. They accompany themselves on the *darabooh*, or tambourine. Their services are engaged for the evening, and the company distribute themselves about the decks; as many as can squeeze themselves into the little cabins.

Amongst the group of vessels to the right may be seen a square-rigged vessel, dressed with flags and lamps: it is called *Arkaba*, and is believed to represent a splendid ship that was used by the ancient Egyptians to carry the young bride to the place of sacrifice. The vessel used on this occasion had a very gorgeous appearance when seen from a distance, like most things Oriental; but upon a nearer approach the delusion vanished, and it turned out to be an old barge resuscitate for the occasion, having been put

through a process of whitewash and afterwards embellished with innumerable arabesques or characters of hieroglyphic species, the work of some aspiring native artist, and evidently laid on with a mop. Similar designs may be seen on the walls of baths, and coffee-houses, and in general exhibit a charming indifference to the laws of uniformity and elegance. The deck of the *Arkaba* is covered in for the convenience of visitors, who are admitted on payment of a small fee. Some men, dressed in women's habiliments, perform dances on a raised platform erected for the purpose. A brass band is also in attendance. This vessel is rowed from Boulak round the island of Rhoda, and eventually moored for the night near the mouth of the canal. During its passage a small fieldpiece is discharged at intervals, and rockets are also fired from its decks. In the morning it returns to Boulak by the same route.

At about midnight the amusements languish, the steamers and other vessels that have been moving about since sunset come to anchor, and some of the revelers are lying about on the decks asleep. On others probably Europeans are still enjoying themselves. A strange and scarcely definable odour is occasionally wafted past of punch probably in course of manufacture by the Franks, and a most decided flavour of stewed onions from the native vessels is tolerably good evidence of the festival being really international and anti-religious.

Silence gradually creeps over the scene. Towards sunrise the dam is nearly cut through, and the men, who have been working hard during the night, clear off. An hour after daylight a salute from the battery announces the arrival of the regent, Prince Ismail Pasha, who, in the absence of his Highness the Viceroy, officiates at the ceremony. Shortly before eight the prince proceeded to a spot overlooking the canal and gave the necessary orders to cut the dam, which being done, the water rushed into the dry bed with tremendous velocity. At this moment some bags of money, the customary offerings, are emptied into the troubled waters, and, as a matter of course, a grand scramble immediately takes place amongst those already struggling in the water and those who recklessly plunge in, regardless alike of life and limb. This scene is the closing act.

## Scene at the Mohammedan Festival of the Bairam at Alexandria
*Illustrated London News,* March 6, 1869

The subject of another sketch is a scene at Alexandria during the popular festival of the Bairam, which lasts three days, following the long fast of the Ramadan. The word *Bairam* is Turkish; in Arabic it is called the *Eed-e'-Sogheir*, and is at the beginning of the month of *Showal*. The Ramadan is a movable fast, changing about 11 ³/₄ every year, and in thirty-three years it passes round the whole circle of the year. While it lasts a gun is fired at sunrise and another at sunset, and from the one gun to the other no Mohammedan will eat, drink, or smoke. It lasts during the whole

of the month of Ramadan, and when it is over there is a general rejoicing, like the carnival of Europe. Near to Pompey's Pillar there were great goings on—a sort of Greenwich Fair on a small scale. The principal attractions seemed to be swings, and merry-go-rounds. The swings were very simple constructions—a piece of plain board suspended with ropes, and on this women, girls, and children sat while a couple of strong men propelled them high into the air. The delight of the younger ones was great, veils flew off and faces were seen, and the owners were helpless; but they did not seem to care much for the broad grins and loud laughs of the bystanders. Some of the older ladies got nervous, and could find no enjoyment from the the anxious desire to hold on to the board, while legs came out in anything but graceful attitudes; but an Eastern lady thinks nothing of her legs being seen; it is the exposing of the face which is disgraceful.

**Procession of the Holy Carpet at Cairo**
*Illustrated London News,* March 6, 1869

Every year there are sent from Cairo two carpets—one goes to Medina as a covering for the tomb of the Prophet, and the other goes to Mecca as a covering for the *Caaba,* or central point of the Mohammedan religion. The *Kisweh el-Nebbee,* or covering of the *Caaba,* is made of black cloth, with a green fringe. The *Kisweh-a l-Toorbeh,* or covering of the Prophet's tomb, is green, with an ornamental border of Arabic inscriptions from the Koran. They are carefully folded up and placed on the camel with the very elaborate canopy of embroidered gold seen in the illustration. So holy are these coverings that when the procession passed there was a rush made at it by the members of the crowd, who madly pressed forward to kiss the golden folds which hung round, and the guards had to use their sticks in defense. There was a vast number of troops out, and some regiments marched before and after the *Mahmal.* The carpets—or curtains, as they ought to be termed—are placed for a few days in the Hussein mosque. They are then removed to the Karamedan, where they are exposed for a day to the inspection of the faithful. On the morning of the ceremony the Viceroy and principal officers of state attend, and the Mahmal and its attendants go three times round the balcony of the Viceroy, when he says, 'Go; and God be with you!' There is a royal salute of guns, and the procession is started on its long pilgrimage. There are flags and standards of every description carried along with it. One man, the *sheikh-el-gamel,* has a function which is hereditary in his family: he rides on a camel, bareheaded and naked to the waist, the whole journey to Mecca and back; he rolls his head of shaggy black hair, and derives a great odour of sanctity from performing the hadj under such fantastic circumstances. Kettle-drums on camels and musicians of all kinds follow in the distance. The women in the crowd greet the procession with a curious sound called the *zarloota.* It is a sound between a whistle and a scream, but it is sweet and liquid like the cooing of doves; and, when the mass of a crowd produce it, a sound as of waters bubbling along a brook floats through the air. If the women's faces were unveiled and one could notice that their mouths were articulating, or if their arms and hands were not hid, one might see some action indicating of what they were doing; but as no such signs are visible, the sounds appear to hover in the air, over and around the pageant.

## Dispatching the *Mahmal*, or Holy Carpet, from Cairo to Mecca
*Illustrated London News*
August 3, 1861

The Viceroy, seeing the difficulties and dangers of the desert route, and the unnecessary waste of human life, not only by sickness and privation, but from the swords and bullets of the many hordes of Bedouins who infest the Arabian plains, directed that the Mahmal should, for its greater security, in future proceed by steamer to Jeddah, and on the morning of the 2nd of June, His Highness in person received the Mahmal and dispatched it to its destination.

A space of ground of convenient size was held by troops composed of a battalion of chasseurs à pied of the Guard, one battalion of grenadiers, some squadrons of cavalry in rear of the latter, and in rear of the chasseurs a battery of six field-pieces was in position, and saluted at given times. The camel bearing the Mahmal is entering; a species of small tent glittering in elaborate gold embroidery screens the sacred fabric from the vulgar gaze. On the second camel is an aged priest, bearing the standard of the Prophet; and on the third is seated a half-witted man, with a profusion of hair upon his head and face. On account of his insanity he is esteemed as a saint, and is known as the *sheikh-el-gamel*. The remainder of the procession (which may be estimated at upwards of 20,000 persons, independent of the mob) is not shown; they were excluded for want of space in the immediate vicinity of the station.

The camel, after perambulating in front of the viceroy's kiosk for some time, was led to a splendidly-decorated railway-car and relieved of its burden. The *mahmal* was then placed in the open space reserved for it in the centre of the car, and the camel (which is also thought something of from his connection with the holy carpet) was accommodated with a truck.

Bags of money were then emptied from His Highness's kiosk amongst the crowd of ecclesiastics and mob in close attendance. A desperate scramble, innumerable combats, and indescribable confusion were the immediate consequences. The bands played with energy; the guns fired; the engine whistled; and the train with its precious charge slowly moved off the platform. His Highness, seemingly highly gratified with the successful manner in which the whole affair passed off, smiled; his courtiers, in duty bound, smiled also; and His Highness then stepped into his own train and was away to Alexandria before one could turn his head.

## Remains of the Railway Embankment on the Alexandria and Cairo Railway
*Illustrated London News,* November 21, 1863

Our sketch represents the appearance of the railway embankment. The tent in the foreground belongs to Messrs. Glass, Elliott, and Company's line of telegraph from Alexandria to Suez. The representatives in Egypt of these eminent contractors lost no time in establishing a station at each end of the break for receiving and forwarding messages by means of fast-sailing boats, so that the public lost very little by the temporary derangement of the telegraphic communication. The position of the operators in such a situation could not be very cheerful or desirable, surrounded by starving peasantry, and in the midst of a waste of waters; but in the interest of the public service men make great sacrifices.

The passenger traffic between Alexandria and Cairo, which was interrupted by the destruction of the railway, was diverted into its former channel—*viz.,* by river; the authorities met their difficulties with becoming promptitude and energy, and speedily organised a daily service of steamers to and from Cairo and Kafr-el-Zayat, the railway continuing to work between Kafr-el-Zayat and Alexandria; so that when the homeward mail arrived at Suez the passengers experienced very little delay in their transit. The engineer has commenced repairing the embankment, and expects to run trains through again in about six weeks.

**The Cholera in Egypt: Inhabitants of Boulak, Cairo, Crowding into Barges on the Nile**
*Illustrated London News,* August 11, 1883

Our illustration shows the scene at Boulak… when the inhabitants, with their sick and dying, were forced to embark in barges on the Nile, for conveyance either up to Tourah, or down to the Barrage… Many of the police were attacked with cholera, and the frequent carrying of uncovered corpses through the streets caused great terror among the city population. This was increased by the public burning of infected clothing and bed-ding, which the ignorant people thought was done by order of the English on purpose to poison the air and to spread the disease.

## The Prince and Princess of Wales in Egypt: Reception of Their Royal Highnesses by the Viceroy of Egypt at Cairo
*Illustrated London News*, February 27, 1869

The royal party arrived at the Viceregal Palace of Kasr-el-Nil at ten minutes past five p.m. The Viceroy, attended by his ministers, received his guests on the platform, thirty yards from the garden entrance. Mr. Reade, late British Consul, his successor, Mr. Rogers, and the consular staff, with Mrs. Stanton and a few other ladies, were present at the reception.

The Prince of Wales wore the scarlet uniform of a general officer, with the star and sash of the Order of the Medjidieh, and the collar and badge of the Order of the Bath. The Viceroy of Egypt wore a blue frock coat, richly laced with gold, and the insignia of the order of the Osmanli. He had a diamon-hilted scimitar by his side. The party went through the garden into the palace, where an address from the English residents was presented. Attached to the palace is a very large barrack, forming three sides of a square, the Nile forming the other side; and here were a fine body of the Viceroy's soldiers and some cavalry lining the inclosure; and it was an animated sight to see the royal party drive off in their carriages with the picturesque zouave uniform of the cavalry escort. The Viceroy having handed the Princess and Prince into their appointed carriage, himself entered, taking the front seat, which was remarked as an extraordinary act of courtesy on his part to his guests. He accompanied them to a palace prepared for their accommodation in the Esbekieh, where, having seen the Prince and Princess comfortably lodged, he left them.

Cairo had been re-decorated and furnished in the most gorgeous style, the interiors presenting a spectacle only to be imagined by reading the marvellous descriptions in the *Arabian Nights*. The retinue of the Sultan numbered some 700 persons. Fuad Pasha, with a large staff, was in attendance upon his Majesty. The Sultan remained two days at Alexandria, visiting all the objects of interest at that place. All the government offices and the inhabitants, both European and native, vied with each other in doing honour to the occasion. The town was brilliantly illuminated every night. On

## Turkish Sultan's Progress Through Cairo
*Illustrated London News,* May 16, 1863

The turkish squadron, with the Royal yachts, arrived at Alexandria on the morning of the 7th ult. [of last month] His Majesty, the Sultan, landed about noon at the Ras el-Tin Palace, and was received by the Viceroy of Egypt and state dignitaries. For some time past, the Egyptian government has been making great preparations for the reception of the august visitor. No expense was spared to make it as magnificent as possible. The palaces placed at the disposal of His Majesty in Alexandria and

the 9th, the Sultan left by a special train, composed of twelve splendid state carriages, for Cairo, where similar honours awaited him. He spent one day in Halim Pasha's beautiful Palace of Shoubrals, and another at the Pyramids, where he spent nearly three hours in carefully examining every object of interest. He also visited Kalals Saidiah, the strong fortification erected by the late Viceroy at the apex of the delta, where the barrage traverses the two branches of the Nile, and which, last year, Sir James Outran examined and pronounced to be a most formidable work. Our engraving illustrates his Majesty's progress through the streets of Cairo.

# Part Three

# The Crisis in Egypt
## *Royalty, Suez & Occupation*

The British attitude towards Egypt was characterized by hypocrisy and indecision from the beginning of high-level political contacts between the two countries. Palmerston, the dominating figure in mid-nineteenth century British foreign policy, was quite capable of describing Mohammed Ali variously as "the waiter in the coffee shop" and "the regenerator of Egypt." It was a trend that was to continue until long after the British had occupied the country. They established what became appositely known as "the Veiled Protectorate," while simultaneously declaring that they had neither the interest or the intention to remain in Egypt for long.

Mohammed Ali was the first ruler of Egypt to employ expatriate "experts" (many of dubious quality), and the habit was continued by his successors to the *pachalik*. The latter additionally succumbed to the allure of Western luxuries and acquired a variety of expensive playthings from abroad, to the applause of the newspapers that congratulated them on their Western tastes. Just as foreign nations waged war in search of empires, Egypt embarked on military adventures in Syria, Abyssinia and the Sudan that contributed in no small part to the squandering of the nation's human and material patrimony.

To consider the Suez Canal as Ismail's plaything may be extreme, for he was under no illusions as to the global significance of the project he inherited from his predecessor, but the excessive junketings of the 1869 opening celebrations were an undeniable self-indulgence. The canal was the effective cause of first the bankruptcy and then the occupation Despite the initial hostility of the British to the whole venture, it was they who subsequently bought the Egyptian stake in the canal, concerned as they were to protect the ever-vital route to India. Once the British and the French were invited in to reclaim Egypt's debt to the canal's bond-holders, the writing was on the wall. The system of dual-control soon claimed Ismail as a victim and emasculated his successor, the Khedive Tewfiq. There was no real sense of an imperial mission to the British occupation of Egypt, which was a unitary state already unlike many previous colonial conquests. France was expected initially to be a partner in what was explained as an attempt to prevent anarchy and to restore the authority of the Khedive, but was really to keep the canal under foreign (preferably British) supervision. The political difficulties of the Third Republic prompted the French to withdraw, and it remained for the British to react to the first nationalist stirrings from a ministry that had been appointed by the Khedive, and the outbreak of violence in Alexandria.

The portrayal in the British press of Ahmed Orabi, the leader of the uprising who espoused the cause of "Egypt for the Egyptians," as a heroic figure mounted on a prancing white stallion or a would-be dictator was necessary for the ego of Empire: a worthy opponent was required. Another boost for the empire's self-perception was the large contingent of Indian troops that were employed in the subsequent campaign. The fact that Orabi's image may have borne little relation to the truth, and that Britain could take little pride in crushing a *fellahin* army in the ensuing combat, was also commented on at the time. Indeed, the pictorial glorification of the war was often contradicted by accompanying texts that urged restraint, condemned the government for its precipitate actions, and warned against the dangers inherent in the pursuit of such a course. It was voices such as these that ensured that Orabi, after the inevitable conclusion of hostilities, was not summarily shot but instead put on trial. The trial, though it was a potential embarrassment to the

Khedive as well as the new *de facto* rulers, and though it was obviously a charade since the whole occasion lasted less than an hour during which the defendant did not speak, represented a success for more moderate opinion in Britain, supported by the newspapers. After Orabi was exiled to Ceylon, the British remained the "power behind the veil" for many years to come. Their positive legacy in the form of irrigation projects, (of which the first Aswan dam was the largest), and a measure of financial stability, have to be set against an unhappy history of long frustrated independence. The last engravings reproduced here show the British coming to terms with the fez and the camel: two symbols of an old order that were soon appropriated by these latest newcomers to rule Egypt.

Royalty

THE PACHA OF EGYPT.

## Mohammed Ali Giving Audience
*Illustrated London News*, May 28, 1842

We have been favoured with a sight of a portrait of Mohammed Ali. As everything connected with this celebrated man is closely connected with the Overland Route from India, illustrated in another page, we have been at some pains to obtain an authentic likeness of the venerable, and, as yet, little understood regenerator of Egypt. Of the personal likeness we are enabled to affirm there can be no doubt, and it is with no small satisfaction we offer this specimen of artistic skill in [our] columns.

## The Reform Club Banquet for Ibrahim Pasha
*Illustrated London News*, July 11, 1846

On Friday the 3rd inst. [of this month], the members of the Reform Club entertained Ibrahim Pasha, and his suite, at a magnificent banquet at the club house in Pall Mall. The dinner was given by the members not only as a mark of their respect for a stranger illustrious alike for his talents and his position, but to do especial honour to him for the facilities afforded to the English traffic during the events in Syria, and for the improvements which have been effected by him and his father in Egypt. The compliment was enhanced by the invitation being conveyed through Sir Charles Napier, and it was at once frankly and warmly accepted.

His Highness, attended by Sami Pasha, Colonel Benfort, M. Nubar, and Major C. Dickson, arrived at the club house in Pall Mall, precisely at ten minutes after seven o'clock, and was received by Viscount Palmerston, Sir Charles Napier, Mr. Bannerman, Mr. Bond, the secretary, etc. The saloon was crowded by the members of the club when the Pasha reached the club house; and the corridor surrounding that splendid apartment was thronged by elegantly-dressed ladies. The band of the Scots Fusilier Guards welcomed the arrival of his Highness by playing the *Sultan's March.*

Sir Charles Napier conducted the illustrious Pasha to the grand dining room, followed by Viscount Palmerston and the leading members of the club, and the suite of His Highness. Edib Effendi, the Turkish *chargé d'affaires*, came shortly afterwards, and was ushered to the drawing room where the Pasha had already arrived.

The arrangements for the event were very complete; and it is scarcely necessary to say, the entertainment was served in a style of consummate splendour. The banquet took place in the spacious dining-room, covers being laid for one hundred and fifty-four guests. The table presented a splendid ensemble , and was principally illuminated from silver candelabra arranged along the centre, alternating with vases of the choicest flowers.

According to Eastern fashion, the centre of the table was filled with grapes, and other choice fruits in profusion. The middle of the room was the seat of honour. Immediately facing His Highness was a large pyramid, bearing drawings of Mohammed Ali and Ibrahim Pasha, and opposite the chairman was a large ship. Our artist has chosen for his illustration this very splendid *coup-d'oeuil.*

The repast was most sumptuous, and did the highest credit to the skill and taste of M. Soyer, the celebrated chef de cuisine.

The members of the club having taken their seats at the table, the Pasha, punctually at half-past seven, passed from the drawing-room to the dining-room of the club. Sir Charles Napier accompanied His Highness. The military band, as the distinguished guests entered the room, struck up *The Roast Beef of Old England.* The band performed a variety of music during the banquet; and on the cloth being removed, a corps of professional vocalists enlivening the party by the singing of glees, etc. On the cloth being removed, the *Non Nobis* was sung, when Sir Charles Napier rose to propose the first toast, "the Queen," which was received with loud cheering, and drunk with the usual honours. "God save the Queen." The next toast was, "Prince Albert, the Prince of Wales, and the rest of the Royal Family." (Three times three).

The chairman then rose to propose the toast of the evening,

"the health of Ibrahim Pasha, and prosperity to Egypt." (Loud cheers). Their illustrious guest was the son of one of the most remarkable men of this age, one who might be characterised as "the great Oriental reformer," and the services he had rendered to his country were beyond all appreciation. As to their guest that evening, every gentleman present must have read the account of the wars in the East, and they well knew the gallantry which their honoured guest had at all time displayed. (Cheers.) They had no business to enter into the policy of the wars in which he had embarked, but whether the policy of those wars was right or wrong, their illustrious guest did right to obey the orders he had received. (Cheers.) He had proved himself a great soldier, and his plans had been attended with great success. But he had another, and perhaps higher, qualification—much as he was to be praised in war, he was in peace an eminent agriculturalist. (Cheers.) ...etc.

Without further preface, he would propose "the health of their illustrious guest, long life and prosperity to him, and might he carry the experience he had gained in this country to the improvement of Egypt." (Loud cheers.)

Drunk with three times three.

Ibrahim Pasha returned thanks. He was gratified with the honour which had been done to him, and he felt most deeply the reception he had met with in that club and in the country. (Cheers.)

Viscount Palmerston rose with great pleasure to propose the next toast. "The health of Mohammed Ali, and prosperity to Egypt." (Loud cheers.) He had been truly a great reformer and a great agriculturalist in Egypt; and he hoped he might add, that though he was an agriculturalist, he was not a protectionist. (Cheers.) His Lordship concluded a most eloquent speech, referring to the character and genius of Mohammed Ali, and the identity of British interests with the prosperity of Egypt; and the toast was drunk with three times three, amidst great cheering.
The Pasha, through his interpreter, returned thanks in the warmest manner for the compliment they had paid to his father, and to the country of his birth. (Cheers.) The prosperity of Egypt was what was nearest to his heart, and he trusted that the close alliance between England and Egypt would conduce to the prosperity of each. (Cheers again and again renewed.)

### His Highness Abbas Pasha, Viceroy of Egypt
*Illustrated London News*, March 27, 1852

His Highness, Abbas Pasha, present Viceroy of Egypt, only son of Toussoun Pasha, and grandson of Mohammed Ali, was born at Jeddah, in the Hedjas, in the month of Siffu, 1229 (A.D. 1813), and is consequently now in his thirty-ninth year. At the age of eighteen months he was brought to Egypt; six months after which he lost his father, who died at Cairo of plague in the sadly memorable visitation of 1815. Until he had attained his seventh year, the child was brought up and acquired the rudiments of an ordinary education in the harem of his mother; when, in consideration of the character and services of his father, he was made a Pasha of Two Tails by the Sultan Mahmoud. At eight years of age, he was sent to the college of Abu Zabel, and subsequently to that of Kahkah, where he received a liberal instruction in the Turkish, Persian, and Arabic languages (with all of which he is critically familiar), and also in mathematics and military engineering. At the age of fifteen, he was removed from collegiate studies, and appointed by Mohammed Ali to the confidential post of provincial inspector, which post he usefully occupied for a period of three years. At this time, the expedition had been sent against Syria, and Abbas was named to the command of the cavalry division of the Egyptian Army under the command of Ahmed Pasha Manickli. His services and activity there were honourably mentioned on three or four occasions in the published gazette. The fatigues of incessant exposure and unhealthy bivouacs brought on an attack of intermittent fever, which necessitated his return to Alexandria. On his arrival Mohammed Ali refused to permit him to rejoin the army, as he required the services at home of confidential men; and Abbas received the appointment of Governor of the Gharbiah district. After two years he was named Inspector-General of the provinces; and during the year in which the great fire in Cairo occurred, he succeeded to the important and responsible offices of *Khahir*, or Chief Minister, and president of the council at Cairo. During his occupation of these posts—for a period of more than eight years—he acquired general respect, both with the natives and European consuls.

The Pasha has always shown the utmost anxiety to promote the interests of the Anglo-Indian transit. He has spent £ 70,000 in making a carriage road across the desert to Suez; he has expended large sums in improving the Nile navigation; and he has now undertaken, at the probable cost of a million sterling, the construction of a railroad from Alexandria to Cairo.

In private life the Pasha is distinguished for his generous remembrance of services rendered during his comparative adversity, and by many other good qualities of heart; but he is by no means free from weakness of character. Contact with the world has greatly contributed to expand the resources of his intellect, and improve the better qualities of his mind. He has been generally misunderstood, and faults and vices have been attributed to him which are libellous and unjust. He is fond of out-of-door sports, and has one of the most valuable collections of horses and dogs existing. He often joins in the gazelle-chase, and in boar hunting, in both of which he exhibits extraordinary skill and activity.

He is much and affectionately attached to his family, and has recently placed his sons under the tutelage of an English gentleman engaged for the purpose, and is generally encouraging the study of our language about his court. His predilections are decidedly English, and he seems to understand the national character much better than it generally is amongst Orientals, with whom the bland and courteous manners of the French commonly prevail.

## Launch of the Iron Steam-yacht *Faid Gihaad*
*Illustrated London News*, January 3, 1852

The launch of this fine steamer, on December 23, from the building-yard of Messrs. C. J. Mare and Co., at Blackwall, was noticed in our journal of last week. We now engrave the ceremony.

The *Faid Gihaad* iron steam-yacht is of the extraordinary size of 2,200 tons, built for His Highness the Pasha of Egypt. It was commenced in the beginning of the present year. She is to be fitted at present in a very elegant style as a yacht, and is pierced with gun ports, and every other requisite to make her a most efficient war steamer.

**His Highness Said Pasha, The Viceroy of Egypt and Koenig Bey, Private Secretary**
*Illustrated London News,* June 28, 1862

Said Pasha is the fourth son of Mohammed Ali, the great pasha. Out of the eighty-three children of Mohammed Ali, four only survived their father, and Said is incontestably the most remarkable of them. Brought up under the eye of his mother, a Circassian by birth, and whose only child he was, Said evinced at an early stage a decided predilection for scientific pursuits, and particularly for astronomy, to which he gave all his time. At thirteen years of age, he embraced the naval career, and it was at that time that an officer of the French Royal Navy, Houssard, commenced the education of the Prince, and passed successively through all the grades of the service until he reached the dignity of admiral of the entire Egyptian fleet.

Said while admiral of the fleet then lived very privately at Kabarri, near Alexandria, dividing his time between his naval occupations and astronomy, his favourite science, when about this time his nephew, Abbas Pasha, died (1854). By this event, Said was called to the throne by virtue of the firman of 1841 which confers the government of Egypt on the members of Mohammed Ali's family. Said assumed the reins of the government on the 17th of July, 1854. A short time afterwards, Said went to Constantinople to receive at the hands of the Sultan his investiture as Viceroy.

One of his first acts was the abolition of slavery; then he suppressed trade monopoly; the capitation taxes; re-organised the army, which he reduced to about 20,000 men; regulated the taxes, commenced and achieved various works of public utility, and warmly supported the Isthmus of Suez project.

At the commencement of the Crimean War, Said Pasha, as a loyal vassal of the Sultan, dispatched to the scene of the conflict an army of 10,000 men, who fought bravely by the side of the Turkish and allied troops.

His energy and activity during his short reign of eight years have enabled him to accomplish colossal reforms, reforms inspired by his intelligent appreciation of European ideas. Indeed, all the establishments originated by himself and by his father are certainly superior to any others in Turkey or in the Orient. Said Pasha has but recently created an Egyptian Museum at Cairo, and placed it under the direction of M. A. Mariette.

## Bathing Kiosk for the Viceroy of Egypt
*Illustrated London News*, October 30, 1858

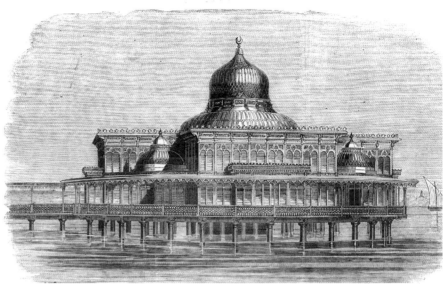

The present Viceroy of Egypt has displayed an enlightened liberality and cultivated taste in his patronage of European arts and manufactures far in advance of most other Eastern princes.

Our engraving represents a bathing kiosk, which is now being constructed in London for His Highness, and which, after having been completely fitted together here, will be shipped in pieces for the Nile. The design has been made at the request of the Pasha. The site for the kiosk is on the Nile at Kafrellais, some distance from the shore, where at high Nile there is a depth of sixty feet, and of thirty feet at low Nile.

The form of the building itself will be that of an equal cross on plan, with projecting portions at each of the four ends. The platform on which the building will stand will be circular and one hundred and twenty feet in diameter, and there will be a circular verandah surrounding the building and projecting from it. There are to be four domes, one over each of the triangular spaces of the cross, and a fifth large double central dome, surmounted by a crescent. In the centre, a square space is to be allotted to the bath. This bath is to be suspended from the centre of the dome by a richly-ornamented chain, which will pass along the top over concealed pulleys, and then be attached to winding machinery — the object being to suit the level of the bath to that of the water of the Nile; and, in order to enter the bath at any level, there will be a square well-staircase surrounding the bath space, which space will be inclosed below the building and under the water by rough plate-glass jalousies. Surrounding this space, also at the platform level, there will be the entrances to the apartments. The various rooms will be lighted during the daytime by windows with glass casements, provided with louvre shutters to shade off the sun, but at night they will be illuminated by elegant chandeliers suspended from the ceiling. The four small projecting portions of the building are to be fitted up as divans. The main part of the building will be of iron and glass, but the interior will be lined with plastering and decorations of appropriate character.

The style is as near an approach as possible to the Saracenic — that is as near as the materials will admit of. The exterior enrichments will be cast from carved patterns, and when erected the lines of all the filigree panels and mouldings will be picked out with colour, the present intention being to pick out the entire exterior of the superstructure with pale blue, white, and gold-leaf. As regards the interior, no doubt a greater variety of colour will be introduced.

All the floors of the apartments will be of the best English encaustic tiles, a material which will be quite new in the country, but admirably adapted to the requirements. Painted glass will be introduced into the domes, and also into the panels of the doors. The interior of the building will be arranged into saloons — the bath space, sleeping-rooms, coffee-preparer's room, pipe-bearer's room, kitchen, guard-room, and a machinery room; in fact there will be all the requisites for the comfort of the visitors, and a more delightful and luxurious summer-house it is presumed cannot well be designed; and if we conceive the brilliancy of an Eastern sun, and the clearness of an Eastern atmosphere, we may imagine the effect of this kiosk glittering with its reflection in the waters of the most classical river in the world. From the shore to the kiosk there will be a bridge-platform supported by columns similar in character to the building itself. There will also be a landing stage, with stairs for the accommodation of parties entering from the Nile.

## Ismail Pasha and the Consuls
*Illustrated London News*, February 14, 1863

The thunder of cannon from the batteries at the citadel on the morning of the 18th ult. announced to the startled inhabitants of Cairo the accession to the viceregal throne of his Highness Prince Ismail Pasha, son of the celebrated warrior, Ibrahim, conqueror of Syria and Arabia. We give an engraving of the reception of the diplomatic corps by the new Viceroy; from a sketch by Mr. Frederick George, of Cairo.

Prince Ismail Pasha has long since devoted himself to the improvement of the old system of agriculture, and has had in view the importance of applying steam wherever it could be made available. His Highness's sugar factory at Rhoda, in the upper country, is the finest in Egypt. Horticulture, in which he displays an elevated and refined taste, has received much attention; and the gardens attached to his private palaces, abounding with the choicest and rarest plants, have no equal.

The Prince's well-known aptitude for business and liberality of character peculiarly fit him for the exalted position he has been called upon to fill, and will, no doubt, lead to the happiest results. It may be confidently said that a new era has dawned upon Egypt.

## Ismail Pasha, Viceroy of Egypt
*Illustrated London News*, July 13, 1867

His Highness Ismail Pasha, Viceroy of Egypt, who arrived in London on Saturday last, is a nephew of the late Viceroy, Said Pasha, who visited this country about six years ago. He was born at Cairo in the Mohammedan year of the Hegira 1248, which is the year 1830 of the Christian era. He is the second of the three sons of Ibrahim Pasha, the redoubtable conqueror of Syria in 1841, when Mohammed Ali, his father, then ruler of Egypt, renounced his vassalage to the Sultan, and threatened not only to make Egypt an independent state, but to deprive the Turkish empire of its most valuable Asiatic provinces. Ismail was sent to France, with his brother, to be educated in the school of the Etat Major, or Military Staff, till his return to Egypt in 1849. These young princes maintained for some time an attitude of opposition to the government of Abbas Pasha, and in 1853 Ismail was accused of being privy to the assassination of one of the court favourites; but this accusation fell to the ground. In 1855 he came again to France on a confidential mission from his uncle, Said Pasha, to the Emperor Napoleon, and on his way home paid a visit to the pope. He afterwards held important offices under the government of Said Pasha, and was appointed regent during the absence of the Viceroy in 1861. At the end of the same year, he took command of an army of 14,000 men for the subjugation of the rebellious tribes on the Sudan frontier, a task which he promptly accomplished. Ismail Pasha succeeded to the viceroyalty in January, 1863. During his reign and that of his predecessor great reforms have been effected in the Egyptian administration, and the development of agriculture and commerce has been extraordinary, which is partly due to the high price of cotton. The present Viceroy, having cultivated that plant to an immense extent on his own estates, is now reckoned one of the richest men in the world. He has taken care to be on the best terms with England and France. Though his prohibition of the forced labour of the Egyptian peasantry in the works of the Suez Canal seemed at one time, three years ago, to check the progress of that great enterprise, the matter was speedily arranged by the influence of the Emperor Napoleon, and the ultimate completion of the canal is no longer doubtful, by which ships will be enabled to pass to and fro between the Mediterranean and the Indian Ocean, to the great advantage of French, Italian, and Greek navigation. The British government, on the other hand, is much indebted to the Viceroy of Egypt for his readiness to grant every accommodation for the conveyance of the Indian mails by the railway from Alexandria to Suez, and latterly for permission to send British troops to India by that route, and to bring them home in the same way after their respective terms of service. These and other civilities on the part of Ismail Pasha have been acknowledged by conferring upon him the rank of Grand Cross of the Order of Bath.

The portrait engraved is from a photograph by the brothers Abdallah, of Constantinople.

## The Revolution in Egypt: Reception of Tewfik at the Citadel
*Illustrated London News*, July 19, 1879

The enforced abdication of Ismail Pasha, Khedive of Egypt, by order of the Sultan at the urgent demand of several European powers, is now an affair of the past; and he has been quietly superseded by his son, Tewfik Pasha, who was hailed as the new Khedive by the government officials, the Mohammedan ecclesiastics, and representatives of foreign nations at Cairo, on Thursday the 26th ult. Our correspondent Mr. George of Cairo, furnishes a sketch of the scene at the citadel, between five and six of the afternoon of that day, when the formal reception was held by Tewfik Pasha. The sketch represents the assemblage of grandees waiting in the anteroom of the palace at the citadel for the arrival of His Highness, who can be seen ascending the stairs in the main court.

**Mohammed Tewfik Pasha, the New Khedive of Egypt**
*Illustrated London News*, August 9, 1879

His Highness Mohammed Tewfik, who has succeeded to the viceroyalty of Egypt, by a decree of the Ottoman Empire upon the forced abdication of his father, Ismail, was born on November 10, 1852. He is the sixth ruler of Egypt in the dynasty of Mohammed Ali Pasha, who was appointed *vali,* or governor in 1806, and who, in 1841, got the Sultan, with the five great powers of Europe, to settle the hereditary principality in his own family. Ali had rebelled against the Sultan, encouraged be the French government of that day, and had made himself absolute master of the country. He was succeeded in 1848 by his son Ibrahim Pasha, who lived but two months after his elevation, The

next ruler, Abbas Pasha, a son of Mohammed Ali's second son, reigned but six years. In 1854 he was strangled by order of the Sultan, as a punishment for attempted treason. Said Pasha, a third son of Mohammed Ali Pasha, succeeded on the death of Abbas; but Said also died in 1863, upon which his nephew Ismail Pasha, second son of Ibrahim became ruler in his turn. This is the Khedive who has recently been deposed, that title being conferred upon him, instead of vali by an imperial firman of 1866. At the same time, the law of succession was altered from that which had been established in 1841. Instead of succession devolving, as heretofore according to the usual principles of Mohammedan law, upon the senior male descendant of the founder of the dynasty, it was to go to Ismail's eldest son, and thenceforth in the same order of primogeniture, excluding the other branches of Mohammed Ali's family. This favour was granted to the late Khedive, in 1866, by Sultan Abdul Aziz, in consideration of a large money payment, but in violation of the ancient and sacred law, and of the convention with the foreign powers. The consequence of that arrangement of 1866, is the present accession of Tewfik, instead of Halim, a fourth son of Mohammed Ali, now about fifty years of age, and reputed a much abler man. The deposition of the Khedive is fresh in our readers' minds, and they do not need to be reminded of the scandalous financial exposures by which it was preceded. A volume just published by Messrs. S. Tinsley and Co., *Egypt Under Ismail Pasha,* Edited by Mr. Blanchard Jerrold, gives a sad account of this recent passage of contemporary history.

Our Cairo correspondent says, "It would be premature to speculate on the prospects of Egypt under the new regime, as the Prince has not hitherto been prominently brought forward. He held office as Minister of the Interior for some time, before the fall of the late Ismail Pasha; but the position gave little scope for displaying his capacity, as he was coupled with a councillor ar adviser, some hard-headed official, who really did the work, and was actually responsible. The Prince's short presidency of the Council of Ministers did not prove a success but he could not have been an independent agent under the circumstances. In private life he is very much esteemed, and is popular among all classes and nationalities. He is a strict and consistent Mohammedan, without being a fanatic; and, though he has not had the advantage of a European education, like his brothers, he is exceedingly well informed and conversant with the topics of the day."

**The Late Khedive of Egypt**
*Illustrated London News*, January 16, 1892

The almost sudden death, on Thursday, January 7th, of Mohammed Tewfik Pasha, Khedive of Egypt, is an event much to be deplored. No Mohammedan ruling prince had merited higher personal esteem, or had more faithfully devoted himself to improve the condition of his people. Mohammed Tewfik, who in 1873 married Princess Emineh, a grandchild of his uncle Abbas Pasha, third Viceroy of Egypt from Mohammed Ali, the founder of the dynasty, is now succeeded by his eldest son. The new Khedive, also named Abbas Pasha, was born on July 1874, 1874, and has been educated partly by English tutors, partly at Vienna. [Abbas is pictured above with his mother.]

SUEZ

## The Suez Canal Works: Excavations at el-Girsh
*Illustrated London News*, February 14, 1863

The illustration of the works at el-Girsh will convey a notion of the nature of some of the difficulties the company has to contend with in cutting the maritime canal. The excavation at this spot is a heavy piece of work, and is evidently intended as experimental. It is cut in the western side of the *rigole de service* to the depth of the proposed grand canal, which is to be 190 feet wide on the water-line. Our artist (Mr. Frederick George, of Cairo) has introduced in the illustration one of the machines employed by the company for clearing the cuttings of sand, where the depth is too great for workmen to carry it away. The arrangement is simple and ingenious. A wooden platform is erected on the side of the cutting, upon which are laid two sets of rails, one on the top and the other on the under timber. Many hundred pairs of wheels, attached to two endless chains, run upon these rails. Each wheel-rod carries a

canvas sack, which can be filled while in transit from any portion of the platform: as the bags reach the top they pass over a cylinder and are emptied, returning on the under set of rails. The whole is put in motion by a small portable engine of six or eight horse power. The saving of time and labour by this simple method must be immense.

The plateau of el-Girsh is about three miles in length, and in some parts has been excavated to the depth of 100 feet to get the proper water-level. The light sandstone through which the cutting is made has to be mined; as, although it crumbles to the touch, it cannot be worked with such implements as the Egyptian *fellahs* are accustomed to use.

The non-professional person is astonished, looking at the works as they are. But when he is told that they are not a tithe of what is to be done he is overwhelmed with the thought.

## Workmen Loading Dromedaries
*Illustrated London News*, March 13, 1869

The engraving on our front page shows one or two groups of the *fellahs*, or native Egyptian labourers, of whom 4,000 are now at work on the canal. They are using camels and don-

keys to carry away the earth from the excavation. Parts of the line have to be constructed in this way by manual labour; the other parts are done by the use of dredging-machines.

## Ismailia and the Freshwater Canal
*Illustrated London News*, February 6, 1864

The sketch by our special artist, is a view of the Fresh Water Canal at Ismailia, with the houses of the Egyptian governor, of M. Ferdinand de Lesseps, manager and president of the Suez Canal Company, and of M. Voisin, or *Voisin Bey*, the engineer-in-chief, agreeably situated on its bank. The châlet of M. de Lesseps is to the left hand; the next house, with oriental arches, is that of his chief engineer; and the governor of Ismailia resides in the mansion beyond. These dwellings have a pleasant look-out over Lake Timsah, a view of which has been given in our journal. The new town of Ismailia, wholly created since 1862, has now more than 6,000 inhabitants, of whom more than a third are Europeans. Two hotels, four or five cafés, a theatre where vaudevilles are performed with spirit, a pretty Roman Catholic chapel, a mosque for Arab workmen, a hospital and a telegraph-office, a long and well-built street with numerous well-stocked shops, a large square, and a public garden planned by French taste and cultivated with French assiduity, a fountain supplied with Nile water; — these are the features which attract the attention of the stranger as he wanders through the town. The rapid increase of vegetation since the fresh water was brought to Ismailia has been attended with a great improvement in the climate. At the present time Ismailia, during eight months of the year, is probably the healthiest spot in Northern Egypt.

### Festival at Ismailia
*Illustrated London News*, March 27, 1869

The subject of this illustration is the scene at Ismailia, on the festival night of Thursday, the 18th, when the Viceroy or Khedive of Egypt, Ismail Pasha, entertained Their Imperial Majesties and Royal Highnesses, with several thousand guests beside, with a sumptuous ball at his new palace on the banks of the canal. The palace, with its gardens, was brilliantly lighted up and thronged with a gay company in a variety of European and oriental costumes; the houses of the town in its neighbourhood were also illuminated, as shown to the left hand in our Artist's sketch. The Arab sheikhs and their followers who had flocked to Ismailia from all parts of Egypt for this grand festival, are seen beneath their open tents in the foreground, serenely puffing the pipe of peace and listening to the music of joy. Three or four European strangers, who have come across from the town, stand there to admire the calm pleasure of these Eastern gentlemen.

### The Empress of the French at Ismailia
*Illustrated London News*, December 11, 1869

Thursday morning showed the strange little town of Ismailia in festive attire. The Empress of the French, the Emperor of Austria, and the other great persons landed early from their ships, and were conducted by the Khedive to his new palace lately built for the occasion. They went in carriages and four, along the avenue from the pier, under a triumphal arch, the road being guarded by two regiments of cavalry, one of lancers on white horses, and the other, with carbines, mounted on bays. They passed over the drawbridge, and turned to the right along the Quay Mohammed Ali, a wide boulevard with the private residences of the principal people on one side, a double roadway with two rows of trees planted down it, and the Fresh Water Canal bounding it on the side towards the lake. Here are the pretty villa which M. de Lesseps has built for his private use, the residences of MM. Borel and Lavalley, the contractors, the house of the Egyptian governor of Ismailia, and the Viceroy's palace. The boundary wall of M. de Lesseps's garden was covered with creepers, and every building was bright with flowers. The best public gardens in the town are those in the Place Champollion and at the waterworks, where the supply of water is pumped for Port Said; and the former was especially gay with evergreen arches and brilliant parterres. The Empress descended at M. de Lesseps'; but, while a number of people were waiting there at one door in hopes of being received by her, she went quietly out by a side entrance, mounted a camel, and rode off along the Quay past the Arab camp. Our front page engraving shows her riding; the Emperor of Austria rides at her right hand, and M. de Lesseps, on a white pony, at her left. She then returned to the palace, entered a pony chaise, with the Emperor of Austria, and was driven about the streets. The Empress wore an enormous straw hat with a long veil, and was dressed very plainly. The street through which they drove is named the Avenue Francis Joseph, and was decorated with a triumphal arch in honour of the Emperor of Austria. The multitude of Arab tents on the esplanade, and the performances of the Bedouin horsemen, galloping to and fro, shouting, and firing off their muskets, seemed to amuse her very much. The Viceroy entertained Their Majesties and Royal Highnesses, at night, with a sumptuous ball in his new palace, attended by several thousand people.

## Blessing the Canal at Port Said in the Presence of the Imperial and Royal Visitors
*Illustrated London News*, December 11, 1869

The ceremony of pronouncing a benediction upon the canal, by the clergy of the Mohammedan, Greek-Catholic, Coptic, and Roman Catholic communions, took place at three o'clock the same afternoon. It was performed in the pavilions erected on the sand of the seashore. The pavilions were three in number, one containing seats for the Khedive and the imperial and royal guests and their immediate attendants, another an altar dressed according to the regulations of the Catholic church, and the third a pulpit for the Mussulman Ulemah. They were all built of wood, prettily carved, and adorned with tropical plants and flowers and the flags of all nations. The masts at the four corners of each pavilion were surmounted with a gilt crescent; but in front of the Christian sanctuary was a shield bearing the cross of Jerusalem, with four small crosses arranged around the large one. The Moslem pulpit, surmounted by an inscription from the Koran, faced eastwards, looking towards Mecca; and the grand pavilion for the visitors fronted both the others… The chief ecclesiastic of the Mohammedan faith, a venerable personage with a flowing white beard, read from his scroll of parchment a prayer to Allah to bestow a blessing on the multitude assembled there, and on the enterprise they had come to dedicate to the service of mankind. This part of the ceremony was very brief, but the scene was a striking one. The Mussulman having concluded, the archbishop of Jerusalem, in full robes, ascended the steps of the high altar in the Christian kiosk and, with the attending priest, said mass.

## The Procession of Ships in the Suez Canal
*Illustrated London News*, February 6, 1864

On November 1st, a procession of some fifty vessels, including the steam-yacht of the Empress of the French, the Emperor of Austria, and the Viceroy, with a Prussian frigate, a Russian vessel of war, various passenger steamboats, pleasure yachts, and merchant ships, went through the northern half of the canal, from Port Said to Ismailia. A part of this procession, which was divided into several detached sections, passing at different hours of the day, is delineated in one of the engravings. The view looks southward, towards Lake Timsah and Ismailia, with the desert stretching far away on each hand, towards the mountains of Sinai on the left, and towards the valley of the Nile on the right. The place shown in the foreground is one of the sta-

tions, which are situated at intervals of five or six miles along the whole line of the canal, where the channel is widened so as to allow vessels to pass each other, and where a few wooden houses are erected, with a small quay for boats to stop at and get fresh water. These stations are all decorated with flags on the opening day. The dredging machines which have been frequently described, were laid up along side the east bank of the canal to be out of the way of passing vessels. The steam-launch, covered with an awning and bearing a flag fore and aft, which is seen coming down the canal in an opposite direction to that of the ships, is the postal boat on its way to Port Said. The largest vessel that passed on this occasion all the way from Port Said to Suez was the Egyptian government steamer *Peluse*, drawing 16 feet of water and 20 feet in length.

### The Breakwater at Port Said, and the Mediterranean Entrance to the Canal
*Illustrated London News*, March 13, 1869

The harbour at Port Said has been constructed by running out into the sea two breakwaters, or moles, which are formed of huge blocks of concrete. Each block measures twelve cubic yards, and weighs twenty-two tons, and is composed of two thirds sand and one third hydraulic lime. The lime is imported from France, the sand is dredged up here in the harbour. Each block cost about £13. They are not laid as in masonry, but thrown down loosely. The breakwaters are intended to answer the double object of protecting vessels from heavy seas and of arresting the alluvium brought down by the river Nile in its passage towards the Bay of Pelusus, so as to prevent its choking up the channel. The western breakwater extends from the shore 2,400 yards in a straight line towards the north, and then with a slight angle towards the east extends 330 yards further. The eastern breakwater leaves the shore at the distance of 1,530 yards of the commencement of the western breakwater, and extends nearly north for a distance of 2,070 yards, at which point it is 760 yards from the western breakwater, and this distance constitutes the width of the entrance.

## The Suez Canal
*Illustrated London News*, July 21, 1883

The last week or two have witnessed the sudden rise of considerable excitement, both among politicians and among
British shipowners and others interested in our Eastern maritime traffic, with regard to the terms of a proposed agreement
between Her Majesty's government and the Suez Canal Company,
represented by M. Ferdinand de Lesseps, the president, for the
construction of a second waterway alongside of the existing canal,
to be aided by an advance of eight million sterling from our government. There is no difference of opinion concerning the utility of
this work, by which the up and down traffic would be enabled to
proceed along parallel lines of canal without obstructing each
other; but many influential persons consider that, in return for the
pecuniary assistance given by Great Britain, the company ought to
be required to make a speedier and larger reduction of its tolls,
about four-fifths of which are levied upon British shipping; that

England ought to have a greater part in the direction and manage-
ment of the company; and that the company's exclusive privileges,
under the concession it obtained from the Egyptian government,
ought not to be extended to a further period of time. These questions will soon come before Parliament, whose assent is needful to
ratify the proposed agreement; but in the meantime, within the last
few days, meetings have been held both in London and in the chief
commercial towns of the North of England, the chambers of commerce have been active, memorials and deputations have
addressed the Ministry, questions and notices of motion have been
brought forward in the House of Commons and the *Times* and
other daily papers have denounced the terms of the arrangement
with extreme severity.

The entire length of the maritime canal is not quite a hundred
miles. The first piece of it from Port Said to Kantara, runs through
the shallow Lake Menzaleh, the bed of which has been excavated
to the required depth along a line of twenty-nine miles, forming a
navigable channel protected by dykes on each side. All this tract of
country is low and flat, being the eastward portion of the Delta
formed by the ancient mouths of the Nile, frequently overflowed,
and half composed of mud, half of lagoons varying in extent at different seasons. Leaving this region of Lake Menzaleh, at Kantara, a
station on the desert route from Egypt to Syria, the course of the
canal for two miles is through low sandhills. It then enters Lake
Ballah, traverses it for a distance of eight miles, and next enters a
deep cutting from al-Ferdane to Lake Timsah. Near al-Guisr, four
miles south of al-Ferdane, the deepest cutting had to be executed,
from sixty feet to seventy feet deep. On the shore of Lake Timsah,
half way from Port Said to Suez, is the new port and little town of
Ismailia, which is the head-quarters of the Suez Canal Company in
Egypt, and the residence of its local managers. It is here that the
Fresh Water Canal, from the Nile below Cairo, approaches the
Maritime Canal, and dispenses part of its water, through pipes laid
along the northern section, to supply the inhabitants of Port Said as
well as the stations and shipping on the Maritime Canal. The
remainder of the course of the Fresh Water Canal winds, and
through the Chalouf cutting, to reach the town of Suez. The
Maritime Canal, however, cuts directly through the rising ground
of Toussoum and the Serapeum; thence passes twenty-four miles
through the Bitter Lakes, which are of sufficient depth, having
been filled by letting in the water of the Mediterranean; finally pen-

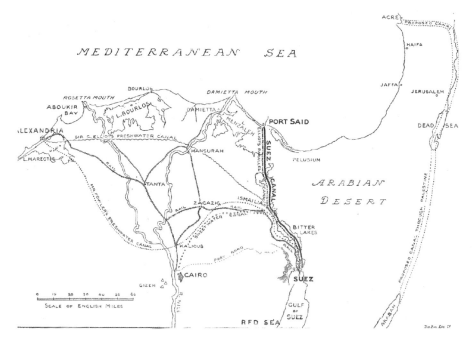

etrates the last piece of high rocky ground by the cutting of Chaloug and twelve miles farther on arrives at the Red Sea, a mile below the town of Suez.

The projector, the creator, and hitherto the supreme director of the Suez Maritime Canal is the Vicomte Ferdinand de Lesseps, one of the most extraordinary men of the age, and whose portrait is most worthy to appear in our journal. He was born at Versailles, in 1805, and was employed in the French consular service in Egypt, in the time of Mohammed Ali, from 1836 to 1840. He was afterwards Consul at Barcelona, next French Minister at Madrid, and in 1849 Special Envoy to Rome, when the French military intervention took place for the restoration of the papal government. In 1854, when Said Pasha became Viceroy of Egypt, M. de Lesseps, who knew him intimately, was invited to pay a visit to Cairo. There, living as an honoured guest in the Viceroy's palace, he conceived the project of the Suez Canal. It was an old idea of Napoleon I, and M. de Lesseps had often turned it over during his former sojourn in Egypt, but without ever having had leisure to study the question in its practical bearings. In a pleasure trip which he made with Mohammed Said from Alexandria

to Cairo across the Libyan Desert, he broached the subject to his host, and the Khedive, perceiving at a glance all the profit which might accrue to Egypt, requested the Frenchman to draw up a memoir. M. de Lesseps set to work, and eighteen months later published his admirably elaborate and yet concise book, *Percement de l'Isthme de Suez*. In this all the advantages that would attend the opening of the canal were exposed luminously, and the material difficulties of the enterprise were so carefully entered into and disposed of, that Mohammed Said, seeing the thing to be decidedly feasible, empowered M. de Lesseps to begin the work. The political obstacles which now beset the eager Frenchman were very formidable. Lord Palmerston, and Sir Stratford Canning (Lord Stratford de Redcliffe) at Constantinople, did all he could to oppose it. No assistance or encouragement was afforded by any influential party or class in England; politicians, set themselves against it. But M. de Lesseps persevered, and the French nation, under the Emperor Napoleon III., entered readily into the scheme, which also found favour in Italy and Austria, and in other Mediterranean States. The *Compagnie Universelle du Canal Maritime de Suez* was thus formed, with an original share capital of eight million sterling; but it raised four million additional by debentures, and received nearly four million from the Viceroy of Egypt as indemnity for his non-fulfillment of some of the conditions of the contract. The canal, with its ports at each end, was to belong to the company for ninety-nine years, from 1869, after which it would revert to the Government. Of the traffic earnings, the Egyptian government was to receive annually fifteen per cent. The Fresh Water Canal was, at first, made the property of the Suez Canal Company, but was afterwards relinquished to the government for a pecuniary compensation. The total cost of the works was seventeen millions sterling.

The work of construction was designed and superintended by French engineers, with two or three Italian assistants. The engineer in chief was M. Voisin, or Voisin Bey. The line was divided into four sections, of which M. Laroche, M. Gioia, M. Berthoult, and M. Larousse, were respectively the resident engineers. The contractors for the canal works were Messrs. Borel, Lavalley, and

Co.; the contractors for the Port Said harbour works, Messrs. Dussaud. The whole was completed in 1869, when the Empress of the French, the Emperor of Austria, and princely representatives of all the great nations of Europe, were present, on November 17 of that year, at the splendid opening ceremony.

Port Said and Suez are the two harbours that form, respectively, the northern or Mediterranean entrance and the southern or Red Sea entrance to the Maritime Canal. Port Said is quite a new creation, being constructed since 1859 expressly for the Canal. The town is built upon an island or sandbank dividing Lake Menzaleh from the Mediterranean Sea. The harbour is entirely artificial, formed by two breakwaters, one a mile long, the other a mile and a half, which were made by casting into the sea about 25,000 blocks of concrete, each weighing above twenty tons. They enclose a space of 570 acres, the outer harbour, which has a depth of twenty-six feet or more, kept clear by constant dredging; three sheltered basins inside constitute the inner harbour. The port of Suez had for many years, before the Suez Canal, been used by the Peninsular and Oriental Company's steamships to India, and by the French Messageries steamers. It was already connected with Alexandria by railway. The works here required for the Suez Canal traffic consisted of a breakwater, 850 yards long, to protect the entrance to the canal; also the deepening of the channel from the anchorage in Suez Roads; and embankments or seawalls to enclose space for docks and basins, including a dry dock, 360 ft. long and 85 ft. wide, constructed by the French Messageries Company.

Such, described in mere outline, are the great works, executed within the past thirty years, by French enterprise and capital, which have chiefly availed for the service of the British mercantile marine, nearly four-fifths of the aggregate tonnage yearly passing through the canal belonging to our own country. In 1875, when the late Khedive, Ismail Pasha, was obliged to raise money by selling his portion of the company's stock, the British government wisely purchased his shares at the price of nearly four millions sterling. These shares, however, do not yet entitle their holders to receive dividends, or to vote among the other shareholders in the company, but they will do after the year 1894. We now come to the recent history of the negotiations which have resulted in the provisional agreement explained in the House of Commons by the chancellor of the exchequer, which is dated July 10, 1833. Sir Charles Rivers Wilson and Sir John Stokes, the two English official directors on

the board, in the months of April, May, and June last, had repeated consultations with M. de Lesseps on the improvement of the canal communication between the Mediterranean and Red Seas, and the conditions under which the canal must be hereafter worked.

The points to which attention was directed were: — 1. The improvement of the canal accommodation across the isthmus, so as to meet the increasing requirements of commercial traffic. 2. A substantial reduction of the dues and tolls. 3. An increased share in the government of the company. Improved communication may be obtained by one of three methods: — (1) By the simple widening and deepening of the present canal. (2) By the construction of a second canal on ground forming part of the company's concession, which would lead to the new channel not being on the most advantageous line; and (3) the construction of the second parallel canal on ground outside the boundary of the company's territory, but which would allow of the channel being traced in the best direction for navigation and for economy of construction. Either of the two first alternatives was open to M. de Lesseps to adopt, without any fresh concession from the Egyptian government, and therefore without the necessity of having recourse to any agreement with Her Majesty's government for their good offices. From the moment that such intervention was rendered possible by an understanding on other points, the third alternative appeared to be the only one deserving of consideration. It is sufficient to mention the obvious advantage resulting from a system which secures to vessels two distinct and efficient routes, one for the outward, and the other for the homeward traffic.

The receipts of the canal for the year 1882 amounted to about £ 2,500,000, of which nearly £ 2,000,000, or four-fifths, was paid by British ships. The year's working expenses were £ 730,000. After certain deductions for the sinking fund and interest on consolidated coupons, there was a net profit of £ 1,260,000. This profit of the year was distributed as follows: — To the Egyptian government, fifteen percent of the net profit, amounting to £900,000. This gives a dividend of 56 francs 22 centimes per ordinary share (of 500 francs), 31 francs 67 centimes to the founders' shares, and 82 francs 73 centimes to the preference shares. There are 400,000 shares in the company, of which 176,602 shares are held by the British government; and these are not entitled to any dividends for twenty-five years in advance from 1869.

# OCCUPATION

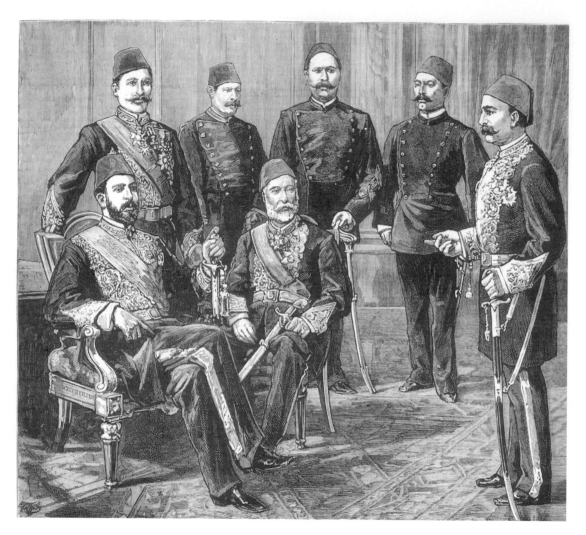

**The Crisis in Egypt: the Khedive and
Some Leaders of the National Party**
The *Graphic*, February 11, 1882

For a whole year, since Arabi Bey and his brother colonels practically mutinied against the Khedive, and imposed on him certain conditions which Tewfik found himself compelled to accept, Egypt has been virtually under the rule of the army, and it seems as though the Mameluke regime is again to be revived. In September, Arabi Bey and his companions once more rose in revolt, and with 4,000 men and thirty guns at their back, demanded further reforms, the dismissal of the ministry, and a constitution. Tewfik, as usual, gave way. Sherif Pasha, the nominee of the Nationalist Party, was named Prime Minister, and an assembly of notables was called together to formulate a constitution. For four months there has been comparative quiet, but the military party have been becoming more and more powerful and arrogant, and the Assembly acting under its influence, could not agree even to Sherif Pasha's scheme for a constitution, but made further demands, such as complete ministerial responsibility to the chamber and parliamentary control over the budget, which the Prime Minister declined to grant. Once more the unfortunate Tewfik was called upon to change his ministry, and again the cabinet has gravitated towards the dictating military party, who may now be regarded as the true sovereigns in Egypt. We publish the portraits of the Khedive, of Sherif Pasha, who has of late won European regard by his strenuous efforts in the cause of organisation and conciliation during his premiership, of Arabi Bey, the talented leader of the War party, of his brother colonels, Ali Fahmi Bey and Abdallah Helmi Pasha, of Fahri Pasha, minister of public instruction, and of Mustapha Pasha, the Minister for Foreign Affairs.

## The Political Crisis in Egypt
*Illustrated London News*, May 27, 1882

The conflict of authority, at Cairo, between the Khedive, Tewfik Pasha, acting under the advice of the British and French governments, whose naval squadrons are at Alexandria, and the ministerial dictator, Arabi Pasha, at the head of the Egyptian army, seems now to be at the most critical point. Arabi Pasha threatens forcible resistance to the demands of the foreign governments, though sanctioned by the Khedive's and the Sultan's orders; he has obliged all the native military officers at Cairo to swear that they will defend his government against any intervention, but the Bedouin sheikhs have refused to take such a pledge. He has also made preparation for defense by sending artillery to the ports of Alexandria and Damietta, laying down torpedoes along the coast, and fortifying the citadel of Cairo. On the other hand, the Khedive, whose resolutions are instigated as well as supported by the French and British Consuls-general, has successfully insisted upon the withdrawal of some acts of the Ministry and chamber of notables, and upon the resignation of the late president of the council, by whom His Highness had been personally insulted. It is believed that a demand has since been made by England and France, or by the Sultan of Turkey at their request, for the deposition of Arabi Pasha from his ministerial office, and from his command of the army; and, further, that he should be sent into exile. It is also believed in diplomatic circles that England and France, in notifying the Porte of the dispatch of a naval expedition to Alexandria, declared that no orders had been given to land troops, and that in case of such a necessity arising the Sultan would be applied to, to furnish the force required of Turkish troops.

Our special artist at Cairo has furnished the sketches of the residence of Arabi Pasha, and of the equipage with which he drives out, with an escort of colonels, to show himself on the public promenade; the figures of some of the soldiery, gendarmes and others in attendance upon the Egyptian dictator, are separately sketched on the same page.

### Rioters at Alexandria Wrecking a Shop
*Illustrated London* News, July 1, 1882

Acorrespondent of our own at Alexandria writes concerning the ferocious attack on the Europeans, that the disturbance began about two o'clock of that Sunday afternoon. "It appears now evident that it was premeditated on the part of the lower class of natives, as groups of them were seen loitering about early in the day, all more or less armed with heavy cudgels. There was a quarrel between a Maltese and an Arab; the latter was stabbed, which caused the mob to assemble and begin the attack. Many Europeans were killed about three o'clock, and then the mob increased rapidly, and began wrecking the shops, which in some cases were defended by the Europeans firing upon their assailants. This exasperated the mob, which was already excited, to a degree of fury approaching madness; and a desperate conflict ensued. No effort was made by either the police or the military guard to put down the riot, and in a few cases they are accused of having aided the mob. The military appeared on the scene about five o'clock, and charged down the streets; both officers and soldiers behaved well during this terrible ordeal. As soon as some sort of tranquillity was restored, the military took charge of the streets, which they still hold: and the authorities have done their utmost to restore confidence. But the terror has been so great, and the complete stoppage to all kinds of business has thrown so many people out of employ, that thousands of destitute Europeans, Maltese, Greeks, and others have left. The exodus is estimated at 30,000 during the week. The commercial and banking houses having closed, the better classes have all left, or are about leaving; the ruin to thousands is appalling, and the native population will feel it as much as the Europeans. It will take Egypt years to recover itself, and certainly not by means of the interference of foreign powers, whoever they may be. As four-fifths of the commerce is in the hands of British houses, you may imagine with what feelings this state of things is regarded by us."

## The Flight from Alexandria
The *Graphic*, July 8, 1882

Ever since the massacre hundreds of families have been panic-stricken, blocking the streets with their goods and chattels in their struggle to reach the boats. All available vehicles have been used, and one incessant stream of men, women, and children of all nationalities, from early morn to night, flows toward the Marina, where there is a rush for the boats; the boatmen charging extortionate rates to take the fugitives to the vessels of refuge, where they can for a time be under the protection of the combined fleets, till the chartered and mail steamers carry them to a place of safety. The sight at the customs house, where my sketch is taken, is one not easily forgotten. The boats, freighted with old men and women, young children, favourite birds, dogs, and cats, household effects of all descriptions and all kinds of odd furniture. One family seemed to cherish a washstand, another an old clock; chairs, tables, bedding, water bottles, all pitched in pell-mell, made up most grotesque boatloads. The fugitives, though many of them utterly ruined, all seemed greatly relieved, and even cheerful, directly they were pushed off from the shore, though hardly knowing whither to go or where to lay their heads.

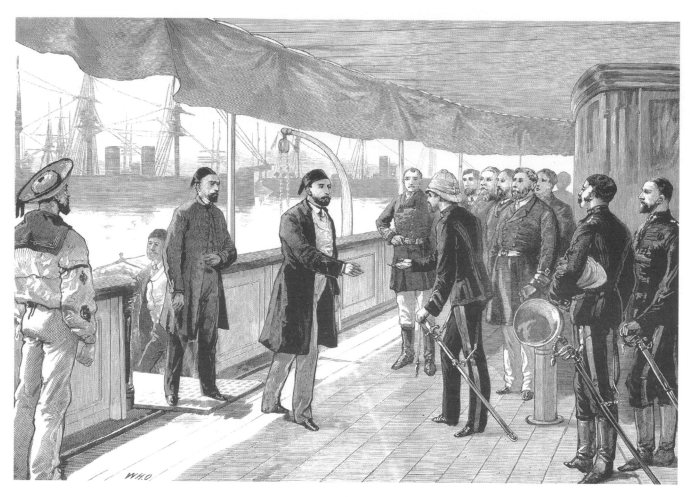

### The Khedive on Board the HMS *Helicon*
*Illustrated London News*, August 26, 1882

At Alexandria, Sherif Pasha has been entrusted with the formation of a new Egyptian ministry. The Khedive announced this in a proclamation, in which he declares that he will himself be president of the council, thinking it necessary in such a crisis that the power of the head of the state should be made manifest to all. Another proclamation issued by the Khedive announces that Sir Garnet Wolseley's military operations are carried on with his sanction as ruler of Egypt.

Among the subjects of our artist's sketches at Alexandria presented this week is that of the Khedive Tewfik Pasha, visiting the Duke of Connaught on board HMS *Helicon*; the Duke of Connaught, who is in command of the guards' brigade, was very actively engaged during several days in examining the country near Ramleh, and in viewing from a distance the position of Arabi Pasha.

## On the Look-out from the Pyramids of Egypt
*Illustrated London News*
August 26, 1882

The Pyramids of Egypt have often been delineated, with the picturesque figures of Bedouin Arabs who are wont to earn money, in peaceful times, by serving as guides or porters to the European tourists, come to visit those mighty monuments of a remote antiquity. They appear, in the engraving on our front page, to be anxiously looking out, beyond Cairo, for the approach of the British army, which may possibly arrive within sight of the Pyramids before another month has elapsed.

The last of the troops hitherto ordered for immediate service in Egypt have left the shores of England, but others are still being sent to form the reserve at Malta and Cyprus. The recent departure of so many of our soldiers from home gives a peculiar interest to the subject of one drawing engraved for this week's publication, in which an English mother, standing at the docks beneath the tall sides of a steam-ship, which is bound to convey some troops to the seat of war, taking a fond leave of her son, a small drummer-boy, whose frame can scarcely be fit to endure the fatigues and hardships of a laborious campaign in a rather trying climate. We shall rejoice to hear of the speedy termination of hostilities, and the return of every regiment with inconsiderable loss of life.

## Bombardment of the Forts at Alexandria
*Illustrated London News*, July 15, 1882

On Tuesday morning, after several weeks of anxious suspense, the attempts to bring about a peaceful settlement of the Egyptian difficulty were interrupted by a terrible conflict between the forts and batteries at Alexandria, under command of Arabi Pasha, and the British naval squadron commanded by Admiral Sir Beauchamp Seymour, occasioned by the Egyptians' conduct in persisting, against repeated prohibitions, to continue their defensive and offensive warlike preparations. The Admiral had discovered on Sunday that there were two new guns mounted on the western side of the entrance to the harbour at Alexandria, whereupon he prepared a proclamation to be posted up, charging the Egyptian authorities with breach of faith, and demanding the surrender of the fortifications within twelve hours. If this were not complied with, he would fire on them after another twenty four hours. The British Consul-General sent a notice to the other Consul-Generals advising them to withdraw all their subjects from the town within twenty four hours. The British Agency and Consular Staff then left and took up their quarters on board the *Tanjore*, one of the Peninsular and Oriental Company's vessels. Mr. Cartwright and Sir Auckland Colvin visited the Khedive, and offered to provide for his safety on board a ship-of-war. He declined, however, to leave the town. The French Consul-General telegraphed to Cairo ordering all Frenchmen to leave, as hostilities were hourly expected. This produced an alarming panic in the town of Alexandria, and the remaining Europeans at once went on board ship. The foreign Consuls made a formal protest against the bombardment. Ragheb Pasha, the Prime Minister, with two of his colleagues, on Monday went aboard the flagship to intercede with the Admiral, but could not answer for the military dictator, Arabi Pasha. There was no sign of a disposition to surrender on his part, and the bombardment was therefore begun at seven o'clock on Tuesday morning.

## The Burning of Alexandria
The *Graphic*, August 5, 1882

The incendiarism and looting which followed the bombardment completely disorganised the ordinary social life of the city. Business was not merely suspended, but absolutely destroyed, there was no work for the labouring class, and the usual supplies of food, by which great cities are every day so quietly and yet so effectively provisioned, were cut off. "To describe the condition of the Grand Square," says the correspondent of the *Times*, "is quite beyond my powers. In the centre, lighted up by a lurid mass of smoke, stood the large equestrian statue of Mohammed Ali;

behind it I could see the Palais de Justice; of the rest I distinguished nothing. On either side of me was one long line of fire. At every moment a house fell with a sound like that of the cannonade of a few days before." Our artist, Mr. Villiers, who visited the square on the Friday evening after the bombardment describes it as "one vast mass of glowing fire. The crashing noise of the falling walls, and the crackling sound of the flames as they leapt and encircled fresh houses, added to the weirdness of the scene."

## The Guards as Equipped for Service

*Illustrated London News*
August 12, 1882

The departure of the Guards last week from London, and their embarkation for conveyance to Egypt, have already been related. Our engraving shows the campaigning attire and outfit of the Grenadier Guards and the Scotch Guards upon this occasion, with their blue spectacles and veils to protect their eyes.

## Arabi Pasha
*Illustrated London News*, July 22, 1882
(Text from the *Graphic*, July 1, 1882)

This remarkable man, who, by that rare quality in a Mussulman, sheer strength of mind, has boldly defied the united authority of England and France, and has made himself for the present, complete master of Egypt and the political situation. He does not waver, but boldly pursues his object, utterly regardless of all obstacles, and in defiance of the prohibition of the European nations hitherto looked upon as the arbiters of Egyptian destinies. In the native opinion, he has achieved unqualified success. He has forced the Khedive to keep him at the head of affairs; he has wrested the internal power from the hands of the Europeans, whose fleets, his followers say, are afraid to take vengeance for the insults which his soldiers have heaped upon them. Moreover, he is now not only countenanced by the Sultan of Turkey, his spiritual as well as his secular ruler, but has even been awarded one of the highest Ottoman decorations — and this at a time when the ambassadors of the great European powers are taking counsel together at Constantinople on the best means of overthrowing him. History alone will show whether Arabi be a pure-minded patriot, as some writers describe him, labouring for the nationalisation of his country, and unscrupulous and ambitious mutineer, aiming at being the successor of Tewfik, as others stigmatise him, or yet again a mere tool of the Sultan, utilized for the long-wished-for restoration of Turkish power in Egypt. Be this as it may, it cannot be denied that Arabi is a man of great determination, and this is evinced by what he has accomplished even since the beginning of the year. Then he was considered to be the most important factor in Egypt, but not even his warmest partisan would have prophesied that in a few months he would venture to defy openly the whole of Europe, and carry on his work of disorganisation under the very guns of a hostile fleet, especially dispatched for the purpose of overawing him.

## The Battle of Tel el Kebir
*Illustrated London News*, October 14, 1882

The despatch of the Commander in Chief, General Sir Garnet Wolseley, which was published last Saturday, supplies the authentic official account of the final and decisive battle that terminated the late war in Egypt. We can provide no more fitting commentary than an abridged version of Sir Garnet's narrative:

"From the daily reconnaissance of the position of Tel el Kebir, it was evident that the enemy's works were of great extent and of formidable character. All the information obtained from spies and prisoners led me to believe that the enemy's force consisted of from sixty to seventy horsed guns, two infantry divisions of about 20,000 men, and three regiments of cavalry, together with about 6,000 Bedouins and irregulars, all under the immediate command of Arabi Pasha. Owing to the numerous detachments I was obliged to make for the defense of my long line of communications, and owing to the losses incurred in previous actions, I could only place in line about 11,000 bayonets, 2,000 sabres and sixty field guns…

I wished to make the battle a final one. I had ascertained that the enemy did not push his outposts far beyond his works at night, and I had good reason to believe that he kept a very bad lookout. These circumstances and the very great reliance I had in the steadiness of our splendid infantry determined me to resort to the extremely difficult operation of a night march, to be followed by an attack, before daylight, on the enemy's position. The result was all I could have wished for.

As soon as it was dark on the evening of the 12th inst. I struck my camp, and the troops moved into position. No fires were allowed, and even smoking was prohibited, and all were ordered to maintain the utmost silence throughout the night's operations. In moving over the desert at night there are no landmarks to guide one's movements; we had consequently to direct our course by the stars… The enemy were completely surprised, and it was not until one or two of their advanced sentries fired their rifles that they realised our close proximity to their works. These were, however, very quickly lined with their infantry, who opened a deafening musketry fire, and their guns came into action immediately. Our troops advanced steadily without firing a shot, in obedience to the orders they had received, and when close to the works, went straight for them, charging with a ringing cheer… The squadron of the 6th Bengal Cavalry did good service in pursuing the enemy through the village of Tel el Kebir, and swept around the northern extremity of their works, charging the enemy's troops as they endeavoured to escape; most of the enemy, however, threw away their arms, and, begging for mercy, were unmolested by our men. To have made them prisoners would have taken up too much time, the cavalry being required for the more important work of pushing on to Cairo."

## The Entry of the Khedive
The *Graphic*, October 14, 1882

The Khedive reentered his capital on September 25th, amid much official pomp and rejoicing. The streets were duly beflagged, and thronged with thousands of natives making the occasion the excuse for a holiday. The station was crowded with officers in gorgeous uniforms, but chief among the personages to greet the Khedive upon his arrival were Sir Garnet Wolseley, the Duke of Connaught, and Sir John Adye. The troops also who lined the streets were British and not Egyptian, while the escort provided for the Khedive's drive through the city was a detachment of our Household Cavalry. Tewfik warmly greeted the British officers, but showed his undisguised contempt at the horde of native officials and *Ulemas*, who a few days previously had been willing to worship Arabi, and were now eager to grovel before their successful sovereign. On perceiving the Sheikh of el Azhar, however, who had remained loyal throughout, he raised his hand in greeting. A short religious service of thanksgiving and prayer was then held, and every *Ulema* prostrated himself at the Khedive's feet as he shouted "Amen." Riaz Pasha stepped forward at the close and shouted "Long live the Khedive!" — a cry dutifully taken up by the crowd, while to the strains of the British National Anthem from the band, the Khedive's carriage, which contained the Duke of Connaught sitting by his side, and Sir Garnet Wolseley and Sir E. Malet facing him, drove to the Ismailia Palace. The crowd behaved itself with that apathy which is one of the chief characteristics of an Oriental mob — no enthusiasm whatever being manifested. At the entry to the palace, before the Khedive arrived, four buffalos were sacrificed, and two more as he entered the gates, the men splashing the blood across the road in front of the carriage. This is the ceremony which is generally observed when a bride first comes to her new home, and is an essential form of welcome.

## Ladies of the Harem Going to the Grand Review of British Troops
*Illustrated London News*
October 21, 1882

A Grand Review of Troops was held before the Khedive in the square in front of the Abdin Palace in Cairo, under the orders of General Sir Garnet Wolseley, on Saturday the 30th ult. The forces assembled were about 18,000 men, including 4,000 cavalry, and sixty guns. They simply marched past the pavilion or grand stand where the Khedive presided. About 500 privileged spectators, chiefly Europeans, were in the adjoining compartments of the grand stand. The Khedive's wife, with other Egyptian ladies of rank, beheld the spectacle from the windows of the harem, and there were many veiled women, in closed carriages, belonging to the upper class citizens of Cairo. One of our artist's sketches represents one of these on the way to see the review.

## Arabi's Trial at Cairo
The *Graphic*, December 23, 1882

The trial of Arabi Pasha took place on Sunday, December 3rd. After some months of delay the Committee of Inquiry into the evidence against the various leaders of the late rebellion in Egypt decided to abandon the primary charges of misusing the flag of truce, and of firing and plundering Alexandria, and merely indict them for rebellion against the Khedive. To this charge, Arabi agreed to plead guilty, and accordingly Ismail Eyoub Pasha, the President of the Committee, reported officially to Raouf Pasha, the President of the Court Martial, that Arabi was duly committed for trial for rebellion, according to article 92 of the Ottoman Military Code, and article 59 of the Ottoman Penal Code. By these it is enacted that persons who revolt, and have disobeyed an order from their superiors to desist, shall be punished with death, the same penalty being awarded to any person who shall retain any military command against the order of the government, and to any commander who keeps his forces under arms after the government has ordered their disbandment. The court accordingly assembled at nine on the morning of the next day, in the large hall of the old Daira Sanieh Palace, where all the political prisoners were con-

fined. As it had been expected that these trials would be somewhat prolonged, the court had been most elaborately fitted up after the model of the French Courts of Justice. The members of the [all Egyptian] court consisted of the president, six generals, a naval officer and a colonel. The audience comprised a number of prominent personages including Sir Rivers Wilson who has watched the case on behalf of the British government. Arabi was brought into court under escort from the adjoining prison, and occupied a place behind his counsel, Mr. Broadley, and the Hon. Mark Napier. He is stated to have lost flesh since his surrender, and to have grown a greyish beard. The president began the proceedings by reading out the charge of rebellion, and asking Arabi whether he pleaded guilty or not guilty. In reply, Mr. Broadley rose and tendered a written plea to the judges as follows: "Of my own free will, and by the advice of my counsel, I plead guilty to the charges now read over to me." The court then retired to consider its decision, and submit it for approval to the Khedive. At 3 p.m. the court reassembled; and Arabi remaining standing in the dock, the clerk of the court pronounced the sentence—that of death for "the crime of rebellion against His Highness the Khedive." Immediately this had been read, the president said: "Ahmed Arabi, you will receive notification of the decree issued by His Highness the Khedive." The decree was then read, and set forth that "whereas we desire, for reasons of our own, to exercise in reference to the said Ahmed Arabi Pasha the right of pardon which appertains to us exclusively, we decree that the penalty of death pronounced is commuted to perpetual exile from Egypt and its dependencies. This pardon will be of no effect, and the said Ahmed Arabi will be liable to the penalty of death, if he enters Egypt or her dependencies." The court then rose, and Arabi *salaamed*, and was conducted to his cell, receiving a bouquet of roses as he passed out from Mrs. Napier. Thus the actual proceedings of the great trial, which had been looked forward to as likely to bring forth some of the most curious revelations in modern Oriental history, and which would implicate personages in high places, and even sovereigns, took practically less than an hour.

## The Camelry Drill
The *Graphic*, November 22, 1884

Our sketches of the Camelry Drill are by a trooper of the 1st Life Guards. The behaviour of this new branch of our service is exciting considerable interest, and the correspondents' letters this week are full of comments upon the organisation and drill of the Camel Corps. "They strike across the desert, and practice advancing in line, wheeling in sections of fours into columns of route, dismounting rapidly—not always at the exact time and manner required—engaging imaginary enemies, and then making off again. The troopers at first regarded their novel steed somewhat askance, but they are now finding out that he has many advantages. Moreover, the camel under British tuition is developing unlooked for intelligence, and has learned the words of command, and pulls up sharply at the cry of "Halt." The process of dismounting and mounting, however, is described as supremely ridiculous. "First," writes the standard correspondent, "officers and men have all to imitate rigorously the gurgle by which their

Arab masters were wont to request their camels to lie down—an uncouth sound which the Anglo-Saxon throat accomplishes with difficulty. Then there is a jogging and kicking of heels and roaring of camels, with English accompaniment; this lasts for a minute or so until, one by one, all have subsided on the ground, when the men get off, and discipline, silence, and military decorum are restored. It is the same when mounting, and, indeed, one can hear a mile away when the Mounted Infantry execute either of these movements, so great is the din, and so loud are the complaints to which the men and the camels give vent."

The Times correspondent gives a graphic description of the "bellowing, roaring, screaming, groaning, and, as the soldiers generally term it 'grousing,' which takes place all day long in the lines of the camelry," and remarks amusingly on the intense astonishment and indignation with which the camel receives any attempt to groom him. In fine, "he is never at any time happy, he will bite at the hand which feeds and tends him… he knows naught of gratitude, is bereft of the softer passions, and looks upon whomsoever approaches him as his bitterest enemy."

## The Review of the Camel Corps at Wadi Halfa
The *Graphic*, February 21, 1891

Wadi Halfa, the Second Cataract, was the limit of His Highness's tour along the course of the Nile. The Khedive was received here, as elsewhere, with much enthusiasm. The principal event of his visit was the review of the troops which guard the frontier from the invasion of the Mahdists.

Our engraving, which is from a sketch by Mr. Reginald Barratt, shows the march past of the Camel Corps, fine, sturdy fellows, who, mounted on their "ships of the desert," made a brave show. His Highness expressed himself very well satisfied with the condition of the frontier. On his return he visited Luxor, and opened a new hospital for Egyptian natives, which has been built from the contributions of English tourists, materially aided by Mr. Brunner, M.P., and Mr. John M. Cook, the famous "personal conductor."

## The New Egyptian Gendarmerie — A British Officer Trying on a Fez
The *Graphic*, March 24, 1883

When in Rome, writes Captain G. D. Giles, of the Egyptian gendarmerie, we must do as Rome does, as the saying is, and so in Egypt, a man must in some case conform to the customs of the Egyptians. The military head-dress of the country is the fez or the *tarboosh* and has to be adopted by foreigners taking military service in Egypt. The fez, though very suitable to the Egyptian, is hardly so to the Englishman, at all events to the officer in the sketch, who is trying one on in the *Lincoln and Bennet's* of Cairo. He is not reassured as to his appearance by the smile on his friend's face, or the evident amusement of the two Arabs who are looking in at the shop door. The fezzes are blocked in a sort of iron mould which is placed over a fire, the outer portion of the mould is removed by two handles, and these moulds on their fireplaces always form a prominent object in a fez maker's shop.

# Chronology

| ORIENT | | OCCIDENT | |
|---|---|---|---|
| 639 | Amr ibn al-As invades Egypt | 1375–1400 | Introduction of woodcut printing into Europe |
| 1516 | Occupation of Egypt by the Ottomans | 1450 | Invention of typography and the Gutenberg Press |
| 1798 | Napoleon invades Egypt | 1712 | Introduction of the Stamp Tax in Britain |
| 1801 | British expel French forces from Egypt | 1760–1820 | Reign of George III |
| 1805 | Mohammed Ali invested as Pasha of Egypt | 1793–1815 | Napoleonic Wars |
| 1807 | Failed British invasion of Egypt | 1809–1828 | Publication of twenty volumes of the *Description de L'Egypte* in France |
| 1811 | Massacre of the Mamluks in the Citadel | 1811–1830 | Regency and reign of George IV |
| 1811–1818 | Mohammed Ali wages war on the Wahabbis | 1814 | Use of first steam-driven stop-cylinder press in Britain |
| 1820 | Occupation of Northern Sudan by Mohammed Ali | | |
| 1824 | Invasion of Greece by Egyptian and Turkish forces | 1822 | Decipherment of hieroglyphs by Champollion |
| 1828 | Withdrawal of Egyptian forces from Greece | 1827 | Niepce's successful heliographic exposure |
| 1829 | Greek independence | 1830 | Palmerston becomes British Foreign Minister |
| 1830 | French engineers build arsenal and fleet for Mohammed Ali in Alexandria | 1830–1837 | Reign of William IV |
| 1831 | Invasion of Syria by Ibrahim Mohammed Ali outlawed by Turkey | 1832 | Great Reform Act, Britain |
| | | 1834 | Abolition of Slavery Act, Britain |
| 1833 | Mohammed Ali reinstated as Pasha of Egypt with possession of Syria | 1836 | Publication of *The Manners and Customs of the Modern Egyptians* by Lane |
| 1835 | Plague in Egypt | 1837 | Accession of Queen Victoria |
| 1838 | Refusal of Britain to recognise the independence of Mohammed Ali | | Invention of the Daguerreotype |
| | | | Publication of *The Manners and Customs of the Ancient Egyptians* by Wilkinson |

| | | | |
|---|---|---|---|
| **1839** | Surrender of Turkish fleet to Mohammed Ali | **1839** | Invention of Fox Talbot's 'Photogenic Drawing Process' |
| **1840** | British and Austrian operations against Ibrahim in Syria | **1840** | Marriage of Queen Victoria to Albert |
| | | | Publication of Lane's translation of *The Thousand and One Nights* |
| **1841** | Evacuation of Syria by Ibrahim | **1841–1843** | Publication of *Excursions Daguerriennes* with the first photographs of Egypt |
| | Agreement to confer the hereditary Pashalik of Egypt on Mohammed Ali | **1840–1842** | Opium War between Britain and China |
| **1842** | Nile flood and cattle plague in Egypt | **1842** | Launch of the *Illustrated London News* |
| **1843** | Plague of locusts in Egypt | **1846** | Ibrahim visits Britain |
| **1845** | Waghorn brings the Bombay Mail to London in 30 days by the "Overland Route" | **1846–1847** | Opening of the new British Museum, London |
| **1847** | Mohammed Ali approves Suez Canal survey by British and French engineers | **1846–1849** | Publication of David Roberts' *Egypt and Nubia* |
| **1848** | Madness and death of Mohammed Ali | **1847** | Exhibition of David Robert's Panorama of Cairo, Leicester Square |
| | Regency and death of Ibrahim | **1848** | The year of revolutions in Europe |
| | Regency and accession of Abbas I | **1851** | Development of the wet collodion photographic process |
| **1851–1856** | Cairo-Alexandria railway built | | The Great Exhibition at the Crystal Palace, London |
| **1854** | Murder of Abbas I and accession of Said | | Accession of Napoleon III in France |
| **1856** | Charter granted to De Lesseps to build the Suez Canal | **1853–1861** | Abolition of the "Taxes on Knowledge" |
| | Visit of Sultan of Turkey to Egypt | **1854** | The Crimean War |
| **1858** | Founding of the Egyptian Museum in Bulac | **1855–1858** | Ministry of Palmerston |
| **1862** | Visit of the Prince of Wales to Egypt | **1857** | China Wars and Indian Mutiny |
| **1863** | Death of Said and accession of Ismail | **1859–1865** | Ministry of Palmerston |
| | Visit of Sultan of Turkey to Egypt | **1861** | Death of Prince Albert |
| **1866** | Establishment of the National Assembly of Delegates | **1861–1865** | American Civil War creates boom in Egypt's cotton exports |
| **1867** | Ismail granted title of "Khedive" by the Sublime Porte | | |

| | | | |
|---|---|---|---|
| **1869** | Opening of the Suez Canal | **1863–1893** | Publication of Lane's *Arabic-English Lexicon* |
| **1874** | Conquest of Darfur Sultanate by Ismail | **1865** | Death of Palmerston |
| **1875** | Sale of the controlling portion of Canal shares by Ismail to Britain | **1865–1867** | Ministry of Disraeli |
| | Abortive attempts to invade Abyssinia by Ismail | **1867** | The Paris International Exposition |
| **1876** | Establishment of the Commission of the Public Debt to service Egypt's debt | **1868–1874** | Ministry of Gladstone |

**1869**  Opening of the Suez Canal

**1874**  Conquest of Darfur Sultanate by Ismail

**1875**  Sale of the controlling portion of Canal shares by Ismail to Britain

Abortive attempts to invade Abyssinia by Ismail

**1876**  Establishment of the Commission of the Public Debt to service Egypt's debt

**1876–1882**  Anglo-French system of dual-control imposed on Egypt

**1879**  Forced deposition and exile of Ismail

Accession of Tewfiq

**1881**  Nationalist uprising led by Ahmed Orabi

**1882**  Riots and British naval bombardment of Alexandria

Occupation of Egypt by Britain

Trial of Orabi, exiled to Ceylon

**1883**  Appointment of Sir Evelyn Baring as British Consul-General in Egypt

**1892**  Death of Tewfiq and accession of Abbas II

**1895**  Death of Ismail in Istanbul

**1901**  Return of Orabi from exile

**1902**  Opening of the First Aswan Dam

**1953**  Declaration of the Republic of Egypt

**1956**  Departure of last British troops from Egypt and election of Nasser as President of the Arab Republic of Egypt

**1863–1893**  Publication of Lane's *Arabic-English Lexicon*

**1865**  Death of Palmerston

**1865–1867**  Ministry of Disraeli

**1867**  The Paris International Exposition

**1868–1874**  Ministry of Gladstone

**1869**  Ismail visits France and Britain

Launch of the *Graphic*

**1874–1880**  Ministry of Disraeli

**1875–1878**  The "Eastern Question" — revolt of Bulgaria and Russo-Turkish War

**1878**  Erection of Cleopatra's Needle on the Thames Embankment

**1878–1880**  Afghan Wars

**1880–1885**  Ministry of Gladstone

**1881**  British defeat in First Boer War

Death of Disraeli

**1885**  Death of Gordon in Khartoum

Resignation of Gladstone

**1890**  First commercial use of half-tone printing screens

**1898**  Death of Gladstone

**1901**  Death of Queen Victoria